A CULINARY HISTORY
of the GREAT
BLACK SWAMP

Buckeye Candy, Bratwurst & Apple Butter

NATHAN CROOK

AMERICAN PALATE

Published by American Palate
A Division of The History Press
Charleston, SC 29403
www.historypress.net

First published 2013

Manufactured in the United States

ISBN 978.1.60949.290.8

Library of Congress CIP data applied for.

For Jessica, Emily and Michelle.
This work is as much yours as mine.

Contents

Foreword

Food is fun, but it is also terribly important. Obviously, it is essential to our physical survival and health. Without it we cannot live. It also does more than that. It carries memories and identity, expresses creativity and individuality, nurtures relationships (or can dissolve them) and connects each of us with our own pasts, places and other people. In a way, it turns humans into cultural and social beings.

A culinary history, then, is not only fun to read but also shows us how people in the past procured their food, preserved it, prepared it and consumed it, as well as what they thought about it—all of which helps to explain what, how and why we eat today. A culinary history of a region can be particularly useful. Regions are a combination of a geographic place, its natural resources and the people who have settled there. Regional foodways—the total network of processes, practices and concepts surrounding food—show us not only how that place has shaped regional culture but also how the people living there have shaped their environment. Regions can be amorphous, though, and are not always easy to define, especially in today's modern world in which food travels—literally and figuratively—across the country. Food can help us recognize regions and understand regions better.

The Great Black Swamp in northwest Ohio is a part of the United States frequently described as the "fly-over region"—that large section of the country between the two coasts whose culture and food are dismissed as bland and boring white bread, meat and potatoes. As you will find in this book, the food culture of the Black Swamp is anything but boring. Although the region has a conservative culture, it contains much more diversity than expected. Also, its food traditions reflect a fascinating history of man versus nature, luck and hard work, canals and railroads, oil booms and industry and technological innovations. The settlement history laid down a layer of primarily German immigrant foodways onto the foundation of Native American and pioneer food culture. It became a culture that embraced scientific, industrial agriculture yet also celebrated the family and home-based food traditions of the past. Although the Great Black Swamp food culture today includes the mass-produced and mass-distributed commercial foods that identify American cooking, it also includes a variety of ethnic, regional and family food traditions.

Writing a culinary history of a region requires particular skills, an open mind and a flexible stomach. Foodways can be either distinctive to or representative of a region. In order to recognize those that are distinctive, the researcher needs to see how they contrast with foodways of other regions. Oftentimes, we participate in regional food without realizing it; it is only when someone unfamiliar with the region points out the uniqueness of something that we recognize it as regional. It helps, then, for the researcher to have traveled—and eaten—widely. Nathan Crook has an ideal background for recognizing regional foods. Abundantly curious about food, he has traveled throughout the country and eaten local foods on every occasion possible. He knows when something is distinctive to a place. When regional foodways are representative of a place—that is, they may be found elsewhere, but they in some way embody the history and culture of a particular place—recognizing them requires getting to know a place and its people in depth. Nathan has done that also, crisscrossing the Black Swamp to attend food festivals and visit home cooks, farmers and restaurants, trying every delicacy offered. This gave him some wonderful experiences and information that is shared here. Even more importantly, though, he found those foodways that hold special memories and meanings for the people who live in the Great Black Swamp.

In today's world of instant communication, ubiquitous mass media and virtual community, regional foods remind us that we all live in specific places. Those environments shape us, but we also shape them. And we need to recognize the impact we have as well as what it would mean to lose them. With that in mind, *A Culinary History of the Great Black Swamp* should whet your appetite to learn more about your own connections between what you eat and the places you have lived.

Lucy M. Long, PhD
Director
Center for Food and Culture

Acknowledgements

I would like to thank the many people who have helped me shape this project. In many ways, this book would not have been possible had it not been for the people who were willing to talk to me, both casually and more formally, about their perspectives on food and the Great Black Swamp. First off, I would like to thank the people who were willing to be interviewed—the voices that speak in this project are theirs.

I would also like to thank Kelli Kling, marketing and events coordinator with the Wood County Historical Center and Museum; Christie M. Weininger, executive director of the Rutherford B. Hayes Presidential Center; Lucy M. Long, executive director of the Center for Food and Culture; and Brian Pickering, whose support and insider knowledge of the area were indispensable. This group shares my interest in local history, contributed significantly to my understanding of local culture and has buoyed my spirits on numerous occasions.

This project would not have been possible without a supportive network of scholars. They have been patient with my constant talking about food, shown an interest in my work, accompanied me to various cultural events and been a sounding board for ideas as well as sources of information and materials. Among the people who gave all those things are Gary Heba, Sam Jaffee and Laura Leventhal of Bowling Green State University; Mike DuBose and Nick Schroeder of the University of Toledo; Neil Shepard and Erica Kubik of Davenport University; Todd Comer, Steve Smith and Doug Fiely of The Defiance College; Elizabeth Mannir of Indiana University–

Purdue University Fort Wayne; Molly Brost of the University of Southern Indiana; Matthew Stiffler of the Arab American National Museum; and Alan Jaffee.

I am very appreciative of the skills and commitment of the librarians at the local public and academic libraries, especially those at Bowling Green State University, The Defiance College, The Ohio State University and the Wood County District Public Library.

I would also like to thank my colleagues at The Ohio State University who have been a constant font of support and encouragement through every phase of this work. You know who you are and have suffered more at my hands than you deserve.

Finally, I would like to thank my parents, Lane and Carlene Crook, and mother-in-law, Judy Luthy, for the years of support and encouragement. Your support means more to me than words can express.

Introduction

Peanut butter, butter, powdered sugar, vanilla extract and chocolate; pork, spices and a natural casing; chopped apples, apple cider and sugar—these items are not unique to the Great Black Swamp. In fact, none of these ingredients is indigenous to northeast Indiana, southeast Michigan or northwest Ohio. With the possible exception of the natural hog casing, most of these ingredients may be procured at finer gas stations and convenience stores across the nation. How, then, do foods prepared using these commonly available ingredients express the culture and culinary traditions of this region? One possible answer might be that when these ingredients are combined in specific ways to prepare buckeye candy, bratwurst and apple butter, we get a taste of the Black Swamp region.

Forces shaping the culinary traditions of the Great Black Swamp region are many. Geography, climate and natural resources all play into determining what foodstuffs are available, whereas the socioeconomics, education, history, background, group association and individual tastes of the people living here help determine what the local inhabitants choose to eat.

Yvonne Lockwood, curator of folklife at the Michigan State University Museum and associate coordinator of the Michigan Traditional Arts Program, suggests that "localized, or regional foods, tend to be associated with geographical locations and often local food traditions are considered by the locals as being natural." Those who see local foods as natural might also consider them to be domestic, trivial, everyday or mundane—that is, until those foods get outside the home and become a commodity or gourmet.

While the symbolic meanings associated with localized or regional foods might only be known by locals, these foods show how attuned to the local traditions and culture an individual is. Moreover, these foods serve as a window into the history of migration to a region and help us recognize how later waves of immigration help influence and shape local and regional perceptions of region and food. According to husband-and-wife folklorists Barbara Shortridge and James Shortridge, common foods are used to emphasize what many may consider unique or representative of the settlement patterns and heritage of the people who live in a specific place for an extended period of time.

To more fully recognize and better appreciate the relationship between food and region, some critical questions to consider are: Who eats this food? What are the processes that this food undergoes to contribute to a deeper understanding of region and place? Where can this food be produced, purchased or otherwise procured? When did this food become significant to the identity of the region? Why this food? And how did this food come to be associated with a specific region? Michael Owen Jones, emeritus professor of culture and performance at UCLA, wrote in a research paper for the American Folklore Society that people "define events through food." He says individuals and groups may also define themselves by the food they prepare, serve and consume.

From the outside, it might seem that there's an absence of strong, recognizable culinary traditions distinctly associated with the Great Black Swamp region of the states of Indiana, Michigan and Ohio. Lucy M. Long, folklorist and executive director of the Center for Food and Culture, observes that regional foods are "complex and often difficult to identify. Frequently, we do not recognize that they are unique until we contrast them with other regions." For example, Texas has Longhorn beef and Tex-Mex cuisine. California may be most recognized for the wine industry and trend-setting cuisines. Georgia is known for peanuts, peaches, pecans, pralines and southern fare; Iowa for corn and hogs; Maryland for blue crabs; and Maine for lobster. The list could go on, but the point here is, as Cary de Witt observes, almost every other state in the Union has recognizable food traditions. On the other hand, as Long points out, Indiana, Michigan and Ohio cuisine is stereotypically viewed from the outside, and frequently perceived from the inside, as mostly bland and boring.

Perceiving specific ingredients, foodstuffs or dishes as carriers of local or regional identity helps define the regional culture, ethnicity and characteristics commonly associated with the population group. For example, across the Midwest, many "local" or "regional" dishes tend to be hearty, minimally seasoned with salt and black pepper, monochromatic—or ranging from beige to yellow to brown—and focused primarily on meat and starches. These types of dishes play up the realm of the familiar when it comes to culinary choices and traditions and tend to be considered family-friendly comfort foods.

While this examination of local history, culture and cuisine is primarily based on information collected from original field research and numerous personal interviews conducted between 2006 and 2013, it is informed by numerous other projects I have worked on during this time: the Northwest Ohio Foodways Traditions Collection Project and Exhibit; the Bowling Green, Ohio Culinary Tourism Trail; and my doctoral dissertation, "Foods That Matter: Constructing Place and Community at Food Festivals in Northwest Ohio." *A Culinary History of the Great Black Swamp* seeks to encourage a better understanding of the influences associated with particular identifiable cuisines and representative foods within these traditions. It also explores the issues of who sets the cultural patterns of how to behave and what to eat in the Black Swamp region. While this book is primarily about the people and the traditions surrounding their culinary choices, it also takes into consideration the historical and natural forces shaping food choices.

In addition, this text seeks to describe the forces shaping the region and the culinary traditions that form out of physical and human circumstances related to immigration and settlement. To do this, an interdisciplinary approach drawing from fields such as history, literature, geography and cultural studies will play into this work on the culinary history of the Black Swamp. While it is not a history of individual places or people, it is a culinary and cultural history of the practices and traditions that are used to identify this area.

The Great Black Swamp was a geographical feature dominating the landscape of the tri-state area of Indiana, Michigan and Ohio from around 25,000 BCE to the late nineteenth century, when settlers drained the swamp and turned its fertile loam into some of the most productive farmland in the nation. While the drainage basin of the swamp was a massive area, the majority of the thickest, densest, wettest portions of the swamp lay within the borders of the state of Ohio. When this area was the American frontier, it was at the center of international and domestic conflicts and was a significant impediment to early settlement in the region and points beyond. This text will explore the culinary history and settlement patterns of both early and late settlers, as well as include current culinary trends that are adding new depth to the landscape.

To add to the base understanding of the forces shaping the culinary history of this region, this text includes numerous recipes collected from historians, cultural producers and home cooks whose patterns of behavior and traditions are representative of the area. It is interested in exploring the processes and products by which individuals construct meaningful relationships between past ways and people. It looks at the ties that bind the individual to his place and his community and the influences that nature, the environment and people have on regional food.

Please join me as we explore the culinary history of the Native Americans, early European settlers (such as the Germans) and later European settlers (such as the Poles, Hungarians and Lebanese) who made their way to the urban centers that grew on the outskirts of the Great Black Swamp. I will also take into account the traditions of more recent immigrants from Mexico and Texas who initially came as migrant workers but stayed to work in the many factories and industries dotting the landscape.

PART I
A Land in Flux

1

Shaping the Landscape

Geography of the Great Black Swamp

Defining the Great Black Swamp as a region is no easy task when one is presented with physical, historical and cultural boundaries that don't always match. While the physical boundaries are the most easily observed and strictly defined, they are also the most conservative and least flexible. The strictest boundaries of the swamp are defined by the beach moraine of ancient Lake Maumee. This area formed the center of the low-lying, densely forested region within the swamp, with a high canopy of trees that blocked the sun. Yet there was a much larger transition zone that was more than twice the size of the area lying inside the beach moraine. This transition zone was also heavily forested with swampy conditions. Of the geographic and cultural boundaries, historical accounts of the vastness of the swamp suggest that the entire densely forested transition zone comprising the drainage basin or watershed of the swamp was often considered to be part of the swamp itself. Finally, the highly flexible cultural boundaries are tied less to the strict geographic or physical definition of the swamp than to the shared sense of commonality contributing to a notion of place and region. In sum, when people perceive common history, values and practices, the strict physical definition of place matters less than common history and experience. To have a better understanding of the food traditions in the Black Swamp region, one must first be aware of the geography complicating the settlement patterns of the region.

The Great Black Swamp was an uninhabitable, densely forested wetland that dominated the landscape of northwest Ohio and extreme northeast Indiana from the end of the Wisconsinan Glaciation Episode (around thirty thousand years ago) until the late nineteenth century, when European and American settlers engineered and constructed a network of clay drainage tiles and hand-dug ditches to drain the swamp. The Wisconsin era carved much of the Great Lakes and exposed a land bridge across the Bering Strait, which allowed the first human inhabitants to reach North America. The grooves left by this glaciation episode can be easily observed on Kelleys Island in Lake Erie. In terms of the geographic location, the Great Black Swamp is an intersection of the Allegheny Mountains, numerous rivers, two of the Great Lakes (Lake Erie and Lake Michigan) and the Great Plains.

Early glacial periods, known as the Nebraskan, Kansan and Illinoian, affected the entire Midwest, but the Wisconsin glacier left the greatest impact on the landscape of the three states that are home to the Great Black Swamp: Indiana, Michigan and Ohio. From around 25,000 to 12,500 years ago, two-thirds of the states of Michigan and Ohio were covered with a sheet of ice one to eight thousand feet thick.

As the Wisconsin glacier retreated, it left portions of the tri-state area of northeast Indiana, southeast Michigan and northwest Ohio as one of the flattest areas of the nation. In large portions of northeast Indiana and northwest Ohio, the landscape remains dominated by a ten-foot-deep glacial depression that came to accommodate a vast inland lake, Lake Maumee, stretching from western New York to Fort Wayne, Indiana. As the glacier continued its retreat, Lake Maumee receded to form Lake Erie, and the swampy area stretching from the southwest shore of Lake Erie to Fort Wayne, Indiana, became known as the Great Black Swamp.

The Great Black Swamp is at the topographical intersection of the Lake Plains that are the remains of ancient Lake Maumee; the Till Plains, which take their name from the glacial till, or debris, left behind as the Wisconsin glacier receded; and the rugged, hilly land of the Allegheny Plateau. Quite literally, this is where the Great Plains converge with the Allegheny Mountains. While there is a diverse landscape on the extreme fringes of the region, the majority of the region is located in the Lake Plains.

Stretching some 120 miles east to west from present-day Sandusky, Ohio, to Fort Wayne, Indiana, the Great Black Swamp ranged between 30 and 40 miles wide from north to south and covered around 1,500 square miles. The swamp was poorly drained by four rivers: the Maumee, the Auglaize, the Portage and the Sandusky. To provide some perspective, the Great Black Swamp covered as much territory as the Florida Everglades. According to regional, nonprofit land conservation organization the Black

Swamp Conservancy, the boundaries of the swamp were created by glacial movement and the debris left behind as the Wisconsin glacier receded:

The Northern Moraine borders what is now the St. Joseph River south from Michigan, across NW Ohio to Fort Wayne, IN. The Southern Moraine borders the St. Mary's River, again running from Ohio to the confluence of the Three Rivers in Fort Wayne. The Maumee River runs through the Swamp area in Defiance County, then creates the Northern Border to Toledo, OH. It covered thousands of square miles, an area almost as large as Connecticut.

The swamp was thick with growths of trees and brush and was long considered uninhabitable. For thousands of years, it was a place the Native Americans avoided except when hunting, gathering and fishing along its streams and rivers. While the swamp was rich with natural resources, many local historians and archaeologists believe that the native bands living in the area before the nineteenth century built their villages on what would be considered the periphery of the swamp—never inside the basin of the swamp itself.

By some historical accounts, the dense swampy lands of the Great Black Swamp stretched north–south from present-day Detroit, Michigan, to Urbana, Ohio, and east–west from Sandusky, Ohio, to Fort Wayne, Indiana, with the worst parts of the swamp being between the Sandusky and Maumee Rivers. To the earliest travelers and inhabitants of this region, there was little distinction between the wettest portions of the swamp and its much broader drainage basin, or watershed.

With the draining of the Great Black Swamp, this region is no longer defined as much by the terrain as it is by the people who have settled in the region. Yet this does not diminish the fact that the swamp helped shape the patterns of settlement of northeast Indiana, southeast Michigan and northwest Ohio. In the wake of the intense deforestation and drainage that occurred during the latter third of the nineteenth century, the geographical boundaries of the swamp would become less important as the inhabitants of the broader region realized they experienced a common existence: they lived at odds with nature and had to constantly struggle against the elements to keep their land farmable.

2

Living Off the Land

Native Americans

B etween fifteen thousand and twelve thousand years ago, the earliest Native American peoples are believed to have entered North America from Eurasia by way of a land bridge connecting the two continents. From there, they spread out across the continent, adapting to the various environments they encountered. Discoveries of stone tools and weapons in an Ohio Valley cave in western Pennsylvania indicate that the first inhabitants of this region, the Paleo-Indian People, were present in the area as early as 13,000 BCE and might have lived in, or visited, the area of the Great Black Swamp as early as twenty thousand years ago.

These people were primarily foragers existing by hunting large game, such as black bears and white-tailed deer, and small game, such as beavers, opossums, rabbits, raccoons and squirrels. Fowl, such as ducks, geese and turkeys, were plentiful, as were fish in nearby lakes and streams. Early natives also gathered what edible, plant-based foods they could from the landscape, such as wild berries, greens, onions, bulbs and tubers. As the mastodon and mammoth disappeared, so did these people.

The first Native American residents in the region were supplanted by the Archaic People, also known as the Glacial Kame People because some buried their dead in the kames—or gravel hills—left by the glaciers. By 1000 BCE, the Archaic inhabitants had also disappeared from the region. Across portions of Indiana and Ohio, the Mississippian Era is characterized by two distinct Native American groups: the Adena and Hopewell Peoples.

Sometime around 1000 to 800 BCE, a more sophisticated culture appeared in the upper Ohio Valley. These people left behind carved artifacts and postholes, suggesting that their sedentary lifestyle supported a population much denser than that of any who had preceded them. Other artifacts, such as copper and seashells, found at Adena sites suggest that they maintained sophisticated trade routes. Moreover, Ohio flint and pipestone along with stone tablets inscribed with stylized Adena figures have been found as far east as Vermont and the Chesapeake Bay and as far west as Wisconsin and the Mississippi Valley.

The Adena People used tools made of stone, animal bone and tortoise shell to grow crops of squash, pumpkins, gourds, sunflowers and maize. They also built effigy mounds, and the Great Serpent Mound in Adams County, Ohio, is America's best-known effigy mound. But before the Adena passed from the scene, sometime between 100 and 300 CE, another mound-building culture, the Hopewell People, made their appearance. The Hopewell relied on farming as well as hunting, fishing and gathering for food. They grew a variety of crops, including squash and corn. They also built exceptional earthworks in geometric forms, such as circles, rectangles and octagons, some of which were used for ceremonial and burial purposes. The mounds they left behind were constructed as burial sites, temples, platforms for religious structures and earthen forts.

Historian George Knepper informs us that in Ohio, the Hopewell People maintained an extensive trade network and exchanged Ohio pipestone and flint for copper nuggets from the Lake Superior region and seashells from the Atlantic and Gulf Coasts. In addition, they secured obsidian and grizzly bear claws from the Rocky Mountains, mica from North Carolina and silver from Ontario. By 600 CE, the Hopewell Culture had all but disappeared from the Ohio Country. Much like the Adena, no one knows what accounted for the Hopewells' demise.

Following the Mississippian Era, two more distinct cultural groups emerged on the southern periphery of the swamp after 1000 CE: the Fort Ancient People occupied southern and central Ohio and central and southeastern Indiana, and the Whittlesey Focus People were found in the northern parts of Indiana and Ohio. Both had improved agricultural skills and built permanent villages with stockade fences. Knepper observes, "For some 15,000 years, prehistoric peoples had lived out their lives in the Ohio Country. Yet they left the land essentially unchanged…they did not cut down the forests, strip the soil, drain the swamps, level the high places, and fill the low, nor did they change the course of river and stream." The passing of the Fort Ancient and Whittlesey Peoples marked the end of this region's prehistory. For nearly a half century following their disappearance, the Ohio Country was uninhabited, which would not be the case with later waves of groups calling the Black Swamp region home.

Native American peoples of the historic period, who included the Wyandottes, Shawnees, Delawares, Miamis, Mingoes and Ottawas, used many of the same tools and grew many of the same crops as the prehistoric Adena, Hopewell and Fort Ancient cultures. The crops included maize, beans, squash, gourds, pumpkins, muskmelons and watermelons. In the inhabitable areas surrounding the swamp, the earliest of the more permanent settlements of the historic period started to appear in the 1730s. During this era, the majority of villages located outside the swamp were on waterways such as the Maumee, Auglaize, Blanchard, Sandusky, Toussaint, Portage, Tiffin, Saint Marys and Saint Joseph Rivers.

The people, called the Hurons by the French and the Wyandottes by the English, were of Iroquoisan linguistic stock and had been driven from their homeland near Ontario by the Iroquois. They brought with them combined methods of the subsistence agriculture based on native farming techniques and foods augmented by new methods that were influenced by the white settlers they encountered. They entered the Black Swamp region from the north, by way of present-day Detroit, and settled in the well-drained yet densely forested regions on the periphery of the swamp near Lower Sandusky on Sandusky Bay and near Upper Sandusky on the headwaters of the Sandusky River, which flows north to Lake Erie.

Sandusky, the place name, is the Anglicization of the Wyandotte word *sa-un-dus-tee*, meaning "water within pools." The 1795 Treaty of Greenville greatly reduced the size of their landholdings and later treaties reduced it further. Yet throughout most of the historic period, the center of Wyandotte power was Upper Sandusky, located northeast of the modern city of that same name.

Northern Michigan was the homeland of the Ottawa, yet they were displaced and also moved south into Indiana and Ohio from the north around 1740. The Ottawa settled only near the well-drained lands beside the Maumee River and its tributaries. Their principal villages were located on the fringes of the Great Black Swamp near Defiance, Ottawa and Toledo in northwestern Ohio and Fort Wayne in northeast Indiana. These permanent villages supported as many as six thousand inhabitants and were located along waterways that helped drain the surrounding landscape to allow for subsistence farming based on the cultivation of corn, beans and squash.

They supplemented their diet by hunting, fishing and gathering from the natural environment.

By 1750, the Lenapes, or Delaware Nation, were forced westward from their ancestral home on the Delaware River in what is now the states of Delaware, New Jersey, New York and Pennsylvania by white expansion and pressure from the Six Nations of the Iroquois. Many Delawares were converted to Christianity by Moravian missionaries who later helped their converts establish villages of Christian Indians in Ohio at Schoenbrunn, Gnadenhutten, Lichtenau and Salem. These villages and their inhabitants were obliterated during the Revolutionary War.

Following the defeat of the Native American Western Lakes Confederacy at the Battle of Fallen Timbers in 1794, near present-day Maumee, Ohio, the Treaty of Greenville of 1795 put an end to the Northwest Indian War and established a boundary between Native American territory and lands open to white settlers. By way of this treaty, access to the fertile streams and forests of the Great Black Swamp was guaranteed to the Native Americans for the hunting and gathering of foodstuffs. Yet the boundary line was frequently disregarded by settlers as they continued to encroach on native lands guaranteed by the treaty. While the 1795 treaty confined the remaining native population to the densely forested swamplands in the northwest corner of the state, this hardly stopped white settlement into these areas. Like so many guarantees made to Native Americans, the promise of this land would not last.

The War of 1812 has been called the second war for American independence, the forgotten war, Mr. Madison's war and a few other names. However, Randall Buchman, emeritus professor of history at The Defiance College, says the period of time leading up to, during and immediately after the war was a watershed period for the natives living in the Black Swamp region: "For Native Americans, the War of 1812 was their last major attempt east of the Mississippi River to stop the Euro-American onslaught into their world." As a result of their involvement in the war, their choices, says Buchman, "became limited to assimilation or moving west."

While the Great Black Swamp would continue to present a formidable obstacle to white settlement, successive treaties chipped away at the area promised to the Native Americans. To illustrate this point, the Treaty of the Maumee Rapids of 1817 erased the natives' title to nearly 4 million acres in Michigan, Indiana and Ohio. Article 11 guaranteed the Indians the right to hunt on the land ceded to the United States, as long as the U.S. government continued to own the land. In addition, the Native Americans were guaranteed, for the same term, "the privilege of making sugar upon the same land, committing no unnecessary waste upon the trees." The area inside Ohio ceded by the natives became known as the Congress Lands.

Even though the treaty guaranteed Native Americans access to hunt, fish and gather in northwest Ohio for as long as the Congress Lands were the property of the United States, in 1820, the legislature of the state of Ohio carved fourteen counties from the lands that had previously been guaranteed by the Treaty of Greenville for Ohio's Native American populations—the Wyandotte (Huron), Seneca (Cayuga), Delaware, Shawnee, Potawatomi, Ottawa and Chippewa tribes. The land was to be surveyed into townships and sold to settlers. After 1820, most of the land was available to pioneers at the price of $1.25 per acre, with an eighty-acre minimum. In effect, this is the official action that forced the majority of the Native American population out of Ohio.

The Wyandottes had cast their lot with the Americans during the War of 1812 and fared better than most of their neighboring nations. Even though their lands were drastically reduced by the 1817 Treaty of Fort Meigs, they maintained their primary village and farms near present-day Upper Sandusky. In return, the U.S. government granted the Wyandotte Nation permanent use of the Grand Reserve at present-day Upper Sandusky. There, farming continued, a school was built and, in 1824, the mission church was constructed by Indians and Methodist missionaries. As a reward for their support of the Americans during the War of 1812, in 1820, the U.S. government gave the Wyandotte Nation both a gristmill and a sawmill that were built along the Sandusky River in Upper Sandusky.

Indian removals began in 1795; however, it wasn't until Andrew Jackson became president that removal actually got underway. Jackson had been negotiating treaties and removal policies with Indian leaders for years before his election as president. And the removal of the Native Americans to the west of the Mississippi River had been a major part of his political agenda in both the 1824 and 1828 presidential elections. While Indian removal was supposed to be voluntary, native leaders were pressured to sign treaties that would give up ancestral lands in exchange for much smaller parcels in the West.

Passed in 1830, the act allowed the U.S. government to move Indian tribes in the East to lands west of the Mississippi. The Indian Removal Act was signed into law by President Andrew Jackson on May 26, 1830. The Removal Act paved the way for the reluctant—and mostly forced—immigration of tens of thousands of American Indians to the West. By the time the removals

Indian Mill in Upper Sandusky, Ohio. *Image courtesy of author.*

began to occur, most of the tribes in Indiana, like the Shawnees and the Weas, had left the state voluntarily, migrating into Canada and Missouri. The only significant tribes remaining were in northern Indiana: the Miamis and the Potawatomis. In November 1838, government agents forcibly removed nearly nine hundred Potawatomi Indians from their homes in Indiana and Michigan to a reservation in Kansas. By 1840, all Ohio Indians had been removed except for the Wyandottes.

By 1842, the Wyandottes were the last organized Native American people to be removed from Ohio. They had lost all of their land east of the Mississippi River and were removed to the Delaware Reservation in present-day Kansas and Oklahoma. By 1850, only a portion of the Potawatomis were left in Michigan and Indiana while a small band of the Miamis were in Indiana. In 1861, the two 1820 mills that had been given to the Wyandotte Nation for its support of the Americans during the War of 1812 were disassembled, and the reclaimed timbers were used to build Indian Mill three hundred yards downriver from where the two mills previously had stood. The present mill building still has a few of the old walnut timbers from the original two mills that were dismantled and rebuilt as Indian Mill.

Native American food traditions in and around the Great Black Swamp are made up of a combination of subsistence agriculture, supplemented with periodic hunting and gathering. Their agricultural practices were informed by a combination of Native American and European agricultural practices, adapted for use in a specific natural environment. Native American farmers planted corn and beans in small mounds of soil and often either pumpkins, squash or melons in the space between. Together, the three vegetables became known as the three sisters.

The native farmers would first soak the corn kernels in water and then plant them in holes three or four feet apart. Often, they would bury rotten fish with the corn kernels and other seeds as fertilizer. The three crops benefited from each other. The corn, or maize, provides a structure for the beans to climb, eliminating the need for poles. The beans provide the nitrogen to the soil that the other plants utilize, and the squash spreads along the ground, blocking the sunlight and helping prevent establishment of weeds.

In addition to multicolored Indian corn, the natives developed varieties of eight- and ten-row corn. They also grew a variety of beans and squash. They developed and grew numerous varieties of beans, including kidney beans, navy or pea beans, pinto beans, great northern marrow beans and yellow-eye beans. Depending on their location, they also grew many other vegetables, including turnips, cabbage, parsnips, sweet potatoes, yams, onions and leeks. Europeans introduced the watermelon and muskmelon into North America in the seventeenth century, and Indians in the interior were growing these fruits within a few years. However, the mainstays of Native American foods in this region were the three sisters.

Across the Black Swamp region, fish—such as walleye, white perch, blue gills, bullheads, crappies, catfish and white bass—were plentiful in the many lakes, rivers and streams, and game was hunted for meat and hides. Like their predecessors, in the fall and winter, the native hunters hunted white-tailed deer and black bear and trapped smaller game such as beaver, turkey, muskrat, raccoon and turtle. Black bears were highly prized for their skins as well as their meat. A four- or five-hundred-pound bear could provide a significant amount of meat, and when the fat was rendered, a black bear yielded a large amount of valuable cooking grease.

Throughout the various seasons of the year, natives of the area went about gathering salt, mushrooms, black cherries, red mulberry, buckeye nuts, butternuts (white walnut), hickory nuts, black walnuts, American filberts or hazelnuts, acorns, persimmons and sap from maple trees to boil down into syrup or sugar. Gathering maple sap was one of their most important mid- to late winter traditions. Typically, the gathering season would start in late January, when the combination of cold nights and warmer days starts the flow of sap in the hard sugar maple (*Acer saccharum*), and would continue until the weather warmed. They could gather sap from the forests surrounding the Great Black Swamp as long as the seasonal freeze-thaw cycle continued. Once the weather warmed and stayed above freezing for more than a week, the quality and volume of sap flowing in the trees would decrease, and sugaring season was over. Once the sap was collected, they would reduce it to syrup or sugar by placing fire-heated stones in a vessel holding the sap or heating the sap over an open fire.

The origin of the use of maple syrup as a sweetener is obscured in history with many nostalgic tales describing possible starting points. According to Robin Mower, it was as early as the mid-1500s that "North American Indians and early European forest travelers drank the clear, barely sweet liquid" of both the sugar maple and the black maple (*Acer nigrum*) as a source of nourishment. Since there is no documentation indicating the origin of the practice, it is impossible to definitively prove or disprove who started gathering maple sap and reducing it down to maple syrup or maple sugar. However, it was probably the Native Americans who were the first to tap, collect and boil the sap into maple syrup and who taught the colonists the method for making syrup.

As various groups moved from place to place, they brought their cultures with them and adapted them to meet their needs in a new environment. In the same way they combined native farming practices with those of the European settlers, as Native Americans moved from region to region, they adapted their lifestyles to suit the realities presented to them in their new environments. Changing their cooking technologies was one of the ways in which they adapted to different landscapes. For generations, the American natives had been in contact and traded with their neighbors and European settlers, and through these interactions, they built up a complex knowledge of their surroundings and an understanding of how to live off the land.

The natives of the Great Black Swamp were refugees, pushed out of their ancestral homelands by myriad forces. As they settled ahead of the European settlers who would follow, the natives continued to carry on as many of their traditions as they could in a new environment. As Native American cooks came in contact with other native people and European settlers, what they ate and the traditional ways in which they prepared food was increasingly informed by new processes. This culinary cross-pollination becomes evident by comparing and contrasting traditional recipes with more contemporary ones.

Some examples of the oldest recipes prepared by the natives in the Black Swamp region are baked beans, succotash and corn soup. Similar to New England–style baked beans, the natives baked beans with maple syrup and bear fat in ceramic pots in the ground. A second traditional food, succotash, meaning "boiled corn kernels," was also common across the eastern woodlands. It was prepared by combining a mixture of half beans and half corn and then cooking it with bear grease. A third traditional bean-and-corn dish was known as corn soup. The cook would take dried Iroquois corn, which had an inedible hull, and then soak the corn in wood ashes and water to remove the hull before adding the corn kernels to beans. Water and bits of meat were added, and the mixture was then cooked into a hearty soup.

It's also useful to remember that the methods or procedures for preparing a traditional dish are as varied as the cook, and Native American cooks were no different. They prepared meals using whatever ingredients they could procure and with the sophistication afforded to them by their level of cultural education, access to ingredients and the degree of care they put into the food's preparation. With that said, many of the following recipes collected for this book have been adapted for home cooks.

TRADITIONAL CORN SOUP

2 cups dehydrated corn
¾ pound cooked salt pork or venison
2 cups cooked beans (red, kidney or pinto)

Cover corn in enough water to cover and soak overnight. The corn will absorb most of the water. Pour corn in stockpot and add enough water to cover corn by one inch. Bring to a boil, and then cover and reduce heat. Simmer for one hour. Add the salt pork or venison and beans. Simmer for one to two more hours. Check frequently to make sure water covers ingredients throughout cooking process. Serves 4 to 8.

CONTEMPORARY CORN SOUP

1 pint grated corn
1 pint hot water
1 quart milk
1 onion, sliced
1 tablespoon flour

2 tablespoons melted butter, plus 1 to 2 additional tablespoons
1 cup heavy cream
Salt and pepper to taste

Add corn and hot water to a medium saucepan and cook over medium heat for 30 minutes. Meanwhile, combine milk and onion in another saucepan and place on medium heat. Let the milk and onion come to a boil. Mix the flour and butter together and add a few tablespoons of the boiling milk, stirring until the mixture is smooth. Then, stir butter-flour mixture into the milk and cook eight minutes. Remove the onion. Strain corn and add to the milk. After cooking for a few minutes, add heavy cream. When thoroughly heated, add a small piece of butter and salt and pepper to taste. A few kernels of popcorn may be dropped on top of each serving of soup. Serves 4 to 8.

CORN AND PUMPKIN SOUP

12 strips bacon, diced
1 cup chopped onion
1 rib celery, chopped
2 tablespoons all-purpose flour
1 (14.5-ounce) can chicken broth
6 cups mashed cooked pumpkin
2 (8.75-ounce) cans cream-style corn
2 cups half-and-half
1 tablespoon minced fresh parsley
1½ teaspoons salt
½ teaspoon pepper
Sour cream, optional

In a large sauté pan, cook bacon over medium heat until crisp. Remove to paper towels; drain pan, reserving two tablespoons drippings. In the drippings, sauté onion and celery until tender. Stir in flour until blended. Gradually stir in broth. Turn heat to high and bring to a boil; cook and stir for two minutes or until slightly thickened. Reduce heat to medium. Stir in the pumpkin, corn, half-and-half, parsley, salt, pepper and bacon. Cook and stir until heated through. Garnish with sour cream if desired. Serves 4 to 8.

Fried Corn

¼ cup bacon drippings
10 ears fresh corn, cleaned and kernels cut from cob
¼ cup milk
1 teaspoon salt
½ teaspoon pepper

In a heavy or iron skillet, heat drippings over medium heat. Add corn and cook for about five minutes. Then add milk, salt and pepper. Cook, stirring frequently, until corn looks done (about 30 minutes). Remove from stove and serve. Serves 4 to 8.

Traditional Indian Pudding

4 cups water
⅓ cup dried fruit
⅓ cup cornmeal
⅓ cup maple syrup, maple sugar or honey
⅓ cup nuts or nut butter
1 teaspoon salt

Cook water, dried fruit and cornmeal in a saucepan for 20 minutes; add maple syrup, nut butter and salt. Pour into greased pudding dish and bake two hours at 350 degrees. Serves 8.

———————◆——————

CONTEMPORARY INDIAN PUDDING

3¼ cups milk
1 cup maple syrup
¼ cup butter
1½ cups cornmeal

1½ cups dried currants
½ teaspoon ground ginger
¼ teaspoon ground nutmeg

Heat oven to 350 degrees. Combine three cups of the milk and the maple syrup in a medium saucepan; heat over medium, stirring to a simmer. Add the butter; stir until melted. Combine the cornmeal, currants, ginger and nutmeg in a small bowl; stir to blend. Gradually stir into the milk mixture. Cook, stirring often, until thickened to the consistency of mush, 10 minutes. Pour the mixture into a greased, eight-inch square baking dish; smooth to even the top. Pour remaining quarter cup of the milk on top. Bake until golden brown, about 30 minutes. Serve hot pudding in warmed bowls. Serves 8.

3

Exploring the Land

French and British Traders

The American Midwest has seen its share of travelers. The French were among the earliest Europeans to travel throughout what is now the American Midwest. The first recorded entry into the region was by French Canadian explorers in 1634. The French exercised a level of influence or control in the area until France ceded the territory to Great Britain in the Treaty of Paris of 1763, which ended the French and Indian War. The Native Americans in the Midwest had traded with the French for generations, and when called on, they supported and fought with the French against the Americans and the British, which put them in a tenuous position at the end of the war.

Initially, the Indians and Europeans engaged in the fur trade. Indians received guns, iron cookware and other desirable items from both the French and the British. In return, the natives of the Midwest provided the French and British traders with animal furs, which Europeans highly desired. The natives also introduced the whites to the vast network of long-established trade routes between various Indian nations. The imported goods of Europe replaced the things they had formerly made for themselves using the resources available in their environment.

Using the same pathways along the Maumee River as those used by Native Americans, French missionaries and traders may have crossed the Great Black Swamp as early as the mid-seventeenth century; however, there are no records of their travels until late in that century. In an article published in 1901 in the *Journal of the Maumee Valley Pioneer Association*, local

Monument to the Great Apple Tree of Defiance, or the French Indian Apple Tree, situated on the north side of the Maumee River in Defiance, Ohio. *Image courtesy of author.*

historian and physician Charles E. Slocum writes, "Along the larger rivers, which were their principal lines of travel, they planted apple trees. Such trees early abounded along the Detroit River and along the Maumee, particularly about Defiance and Fort Wayne."

Of all the apple trees planted by the French traders, one in particular rose to particular prominence: the French Indian Apple Tree, also known as the Old Apple Tree or the Great Apple Tree of Defiance. Widely considered to have been planted by the French in 1670, this tree on the north bank of the Maumee provided apples to travelers, traders and Native Americans living across the river in the Shawnee villages of Chief Blue Jacket for many years. It was spared by General "Mad" Anthony Wayne when he ordered Fort Defiance to be built at the confluence of the Auglaize and Maumee Rivers in August 1794 in advance of the Northwest Indian War's Battle of Fallen Timbers on August 20, 1794. Following the Battle of Fallen Timbers, the tree was also spared when Wayne ordered the destruction of all Native American villages and their crops within a fifty-mile radius of Fort Defiance.

As tensions ramped up between the British and Americans in advance of the War of 1812, the Great Apple Tree of Defiance continued bearing apples. As the Native Americans were removed and American settlers began to slowly populate the area that would eventually come to be known as Defiance, Ohio, the tree continued to bear fruit.

In 1860, Benson J. Lossing, historian and author of the book *Pictorial Field Book of the War of 1812*, visited Defiance, measured the "aged and gigantic tree" and recorded it as "the Largest Apple Tree in America." Even though the trunk was splitting under the weight of the three main branches and decay had already started to set in, the "venerable tree measured twenty-one feet and nine inches in circumference, four feet above the ground"; and it was "upwards of forty-five feet in height and shed apples some distance all around the outside of a circular fence fifty-eight feet in diameter which surrounded it between the years 1853 and 1864." The fact that, according to the monument placed at the site of the Great Apple Tree in 1872, this tree bore two hundred bushels of apples in a single year lends some perspective to what a tree this age and size is capable of producing. Despite the incredible harvest, the tree was entering a period of rapid decay, and one of the three main branches fell to the ground in 1875. The last of the larger branches came down in 1887.

When control of the territory passed from the French to the British, the Native Americans were concerned that if the Americans were to gain control of the region, there would be a flood of white settlers east of the Alleghenies, and many of the native tribes shifted their alliances from France toward Great Britain. To secure Britain's alliances with the natives, King George III issued the Royal Proclamation of 1763, which sought to maintain peace with the indigenous people by regulating trade and prohibiting white settlement west of the Alleghenies. The Royal Proclamation of 1763 ceased to be law when the Americans received their independence following the American Revolution that ended with the Treaty of Paris of 1783. While control of the vast country west of the Alleghenies would pass from the British to the Americans, border skirmishes between the British and Americans would continue to impede settlement. During this time, the British incited the natives into making raids on the sparse American settlements throughout the area that would become the Northwest Territory.

4
Shifting Control of the Land

The Americans Take Over

By July 1787, the Congress of the Confederation of the United States unanimously passed the Northwest Ordinance, which created the Northwest Territory and established the precedent for the U.S.'s westward expansion across North America by the admission of new states, rather than by the expansion of existing states. Up until this point, the states of Connecticut, New York, Pennsylvania and Virginia had—often overlapping—land grants stretching back to the colonial period, and these would continue to influence the settlement patterns of the future states.

Settlement across the Northwest Territory would be achieved in stages, over multiple generations and with most of the land grants claiming portions of the Midwest relinquished early on. Of all the states holding claim to settlement rights in the Northwest Territory, Connecticut and Virginia continued to hold the strongest claims to land. Settlers from these states would carve communities first from the forests of Ohio and then Indiana and Michigan. For example, the Connecticut Western Reserve, parts of which are also known as the Firelands, is located across northern Ohio and Indiana. Large portions of the reserve in the northeast portion of Ohio were settled mainly by New Englanders and their descendants who lost their homes and farms in the American Revolution.

The Virginia Military Bounty Lands of southern Ohio were granted to veterans of the Revolution from Virginia. Stretching like an inverted V shape from the Ohio River in southern Ohio into central Ohio, the Virginia Military Bounty Lands tend to be culturally associated with the South and the states carved from the Dominion and Colony of Virginia: Virginia, West Virginia and Kentucky.

In 1788, the first forty-eight men of the Ohio Company left Massachusetts and Connecticut to follow Generals Rufus Putnam and Benjamin Tupper's invitation to claim land in the Ohio Country as payment for their support and participation in the American Revolutionary War. On July 4, 1788, they held the first dinner in Marietta, celebrating their accomplishments in the Ohio wilderness. Within a generation, what started with a single company of settlers would swell exponentially and push the native peoples farther and farther west.

On March 1, 1803, Ohio was the first state out of the Northwest Territory admitted into the Union. Indiana would follow the path to statehood on December 11, 1816, and Michigan would be granted statehood on January 26, 1837. Yet, the British would continue to have a presence until 1815, the end of the War of 1812. Often considered by historians to be the end of the American Revolution, the War of 1812 was a thirty-two-month military and political conflict fought on three primary frontiers: the Atlantic seaboard, the Gulf Coast and along the Great Lakes and waterways separating the American-Canadian frontier.

The decisive battle of the war on the Great Lakes was the Battle of Lake Erie on September 10, 1813. Under his personal battle flag "Don't Give Up the Ship"—commemorating the dying command of his dear friend and mentor, Captain James Lawrence, who was killed in a single-ship action in 1813 aboard the USS *Chesapeake*—Commodore Oliver Hazard Perry, namesake of Perrysburg, Ohio, and the American fleet outnumbered, engaged and defeated the British near Put-in-Bay. Perry's flagship, the USS *Lawrence*, was so severely disabled in the encounter that he had the flag pulled and his men row him a half mile through heavy gunfire to transfer his command to the USS *Niagara*. After Perry's hard-fought battle, he hastily penned a note on the back of an envelope letting General William Henry Harrison know that "we have met the enemy and they are ours." This victory made it possible for the American Army of the Northwest under Harrison's command to be ferried across the Detroit River to Windsor, Ontario, to pursue the British to defeat at the Battle of the Thames near present-day Chatham, Ontario, on October 5, 1813. It resulted in the death of the Shawnee chief Tecumseh and the destruction of the Native American coalition that he led. These two battles are the reason the Black Swamp region is still part of the United States and not Britain.

While the Black Swamp region was the last portion of the tri-state area of Indiana, Michigan and Ohio to be settled, settlers bound for other areas of the Northwest Territory had to circumnavigate the inhospitable landscape of the swamp. Anyone heading north to Michigan, west to Indiana or Illinois or northwest toward Wisconsin or Minnesota had to travel either around or through the dense forest, swamps and marshes of the Great Black Swamp. Because of the time involved with going around the swamp and the hardships caused by going through it, a plan was hatched to develop a federal road that would help settlers and the Army of the Old Northwest travel through the swamp. In 1808, the U.S. government obtained a strip of land from the Native Americans to build the Maumee and Western Reserve Road through the area. When it was completed in 1827, the poorly designed, 120-foot-wide swath through the dense forest was cleared of trees but was little more than a mud road that was so difficult to pass, travelers often only made a mile's progress each day of their trek through the swamp. By 1835, the road's conditions had deteriorated to the point that it was billed as the "Worst Road on the Continent." Today, U.S. Highway 20 follows the same route and connects Boston, Massachusetts, to Newport, Oregon, with many points in between.

5

Naming the Land

The Great Black Swamp

B y the beginning of the second decade of the nineteenth century, the Midwest was at the center of international conflict and politics. During this early period of American expansion across the landscape, the swamp presented a daunting and often terrifying barrier to anyone traveling from the eastern states through the young state of Ohio and into territories of Michigan, Indiana, Illinois and other parts of the Old Northwest Territory.

With the outbreak of hostilities with the British in 1812, President James Madison put General William Hull in charge of the Army of the Northwest. Hull had been appointed as the first territorial governor of Michigan by President Thomas Jefferson in 1805, and he was now given the responsibility of defending Fort Detroit and the Old Northwest Territory against British invasion. In order to move two thousand American troops from Fort Findlay, near present-day Findlay, Ohio, into the Michigan Territory, Hull had three routes available to him. The first, by water, was the most common route, which would require transport by way of Lake Erie up the Maumee River. The downside to using this route was that the British navy controlled the majority of Lake Erie and using it would alert the British to the movement of American troops.

The second route, by land, would require troops to march out and around the southern perimeter of the swamp, west across northwest Ohio, into the Indiana Territory to Fort Wayne and then north-northeast toward Detroit. This route would require significantly more time to move troops into place.

View of Historic Fort Wayne at the headwaters of the Maumee River in Fort Wayne, Indiana. *Image courtesy of author.*

The third route, also by land, called for American troops to be moved directly north from Fort Findlay, through the swamp to the Maumee Rapids and then northeast to Fort Detroit.

Not only would this third route require Hull's army to cut and clear the roadway of brush, trees and stumps through the dense primeval forest that stretched across northwest Ohio and southern Michigan, but it would also require stabilizing a roadbed so wagons and heavy artillery could pass through the center of the impenetrable Great Black Swamp. During the months of June and July 1812, some two thousand American troops under the command of General William Hull hastily cut a rough passage through the heavy timber of northwest Ohio and southeast Michigan.

In his journal, Joseph Badger, the first missionary in the Connecticut Western Reserve, referred to the "hideous swamps" and wrote about the problems facing General Hull's army: "Man and horse had to travel mid-leg deep in mud and the mud was deep in our tents." With the outbreak of the War of 1812, Badger became a chaplain for soldiers in Ohio, as well as a postmaster for the men in the army. After the war, Badger settled in the swamp near Perrysburg, Ohio, and remained there until he died in 1847.

Lieutenant Eleazer D. Wood, American army officer during the War of 1812, describes the area: "These two rivers: the Maumee and Sandusky,

View of the Portage River at William Henry Harrison Park, where around 1,700 troops of the Army of the Northwest, under the command of General Harrison, spent the winter of 1812–13, near present-day Pemberville, Ohio. Once the swamp froze over, Harrison led the troops to the rapids of the Maumee River, where construction of Fort Meigs began. *Image courtesy of author*.

Low-angle view of Fort Meigs from the Maumee River. Perrysburg, Ohio. *Image courtesy of author*.

are 36 miles apart, and the country which lies between them is almost an entire marsh, or sunken swamp; with an immense body of water [that] can scarcely be passed at any time other than summer or winter, after its waters are sufficiently frozen to bear the traveler." During the war, Wood was promoted first to captain and then to lieutenant colonel and placed in command of the Twenty-first Infantry Regiment. While participating in the defense of Fort Erie in Ontario, Canada, Colonel Wood was killed in a sortie on September 17, 1814. Wood is the namesake of the first county organized in the swamp, Wood County, Ohio. He is also the namesake of Fort Wood, the star-shaped fortification on Bedloe's Island (now Liberty Island) in New York Harbor on which the Statue of Liberty was built.

Hull's army built a corduroy road using the trees it felled and then laid crosswise across the road to let the trees absorb the moisture and mud until a firm roadbed was achieved. In some especially wet areas, multiple layers of logs were necessary. Using this method of road building, Hull's troops were able to stabilize the swampy areas enough to build a serviceable yet bone-jarring roadbed, barely wide enough to enable the Army of the Northwest to pass with its wagons, artillery and supplies.

Robert Lucas, future governor of the state of Ohio and namesake of Lucas County, Ohio, recalls, "It was a very rainy day" when he set out from the foot of the Maumee Rapids, near where Fort Meigs would be built, to join the Army of the Northwest general William Hull's forces, who were assembling in Urbana, Ohio. Urbana was a frontier outpost a little more than one hundred miles south of his starting point near present-day Perrysburg, Ohio. Lucas's journey would take him due south down the newly cut military road, directly through a swampy, densely forested wilderness that European and American explorers referred to as the Maumee Swamp or the Big Swamp.

In his journal entry dated June 10, 1812, Lucas writes about his experiences crossing the wilderness and offers what may be the first recorded reference to the Black Swamp by that name: "Started from the foot of the Rapids to meet the army proceeded through the wilderness toward Urbana—traveled ab[o]ut 25 miles, a very rainy day and then encamped in what is Called the Black Swamp, had a Disagreeable night of wet and Musketoes."

Two natural features may offer explanations for the name the Great Black Swamp. The first is the dark color of the soil, and the second is the dark shade beneath the dense canopy of the trees.

Before long, the international tensions that brought Robert Lucas to this part of the Old Northwest Territory would redirect national attention toward

War of 1812 reenactors at Fort Meigs being served a midday meal of baked ham and turkey, fresh baked bread, dressing and roasted apples. Perrysburg, Ohio. *Image courtesy of author.*

one of the most inhospitable places that early Americans had encountered in the expansion west of the Alleghenies: the Great Black Swamp.

Also known as Hull's Trace, Hull's Military Road holds the distinction of being both the first military road and the first federally constructed and maintained road in the United States. As Lyle Fletcher, emeritus professor of geography at Bowling Green State University and cofounder of the Wood County Historical Society, describes, historically, the full two-hundred-mile length started in Urbana, around forty miles northeast of Dayton. It then made its way north to Fort Findlay and entered the southern edge of the swamp "south of North Baltimore, continued north through the eastern section of that present little city, ran just west of now Cygnet, and from the Portage blockhouse veered east, ran through Bowling Green near the western edge of the Bowling Green State University grounds and crossed the Maumee about two miles south of Maumee City."

Exiting the Great Black Swamp at Maumee, Ohio, the road proceeded northeast toward present-day Toledo and then north to Fort Detroit.

As the tension between the Americans and British increased, in early August 1812, British forces under the command of General Isaac Brock encamped near present-day Windsor, Ontario. Brock ordered his artillery battery to be set up directly across the Detroit River and trained on Fort Detroit. With the cannons in place, Brock threatened Hull with a massacre at the hands of his artillery and his Native American allies if Hull did not give up the fort. Unable to remove Hull from his fortifications, Brock ordered an invasion. Even though Hull's forces outnumbered the enemy, as casualties started to mount, Hull feared an impending massacre. On August 16, 1812, General William Hull surrendered the fort, all weapons, troops under his command and American interests in and around Detroit instead of going into battle. Robert Lucas, the soldier who first recorded the name of the Great Black Swamp in his journal, was a witness to the surrender.

At the outbreak of the War of 1812, Indiana and Michigan were sparsely populated by white settlers, and the only white settlements in northwest Ohio were located at the Maumee Rapids (Perrysburg) and Lower Sandusky (present-day Fremont, Ohio). Although other parts of Ohio were well populated with major settlements along the Ohio River, as well as throughout the interior of the state, the northwest section was not. When news of Hull's surrender reached these secluded wilderness outposts, panic ensued, and the settlers abandoned their farms and homes, fleeing east. It was soon after that the Native American allies of the British set fire to these small settlements in the northwest Ohio wilderness. Hostilities between the Americans and the British ceased shortly after the signing of the Treaty of Ghent in 1815, and American settlement in northern Ohio, Michigan and Indiana started to increase. However, the Great Black Swamp continued to be a major geographical impediment to settlement. During this period, Hull's Trace continued to be the primary north–south route through northwest Ohio.

Soon after the first county within the swamp—Wood County—was formally established in northwest Ohio in 1820, the newly elected county commissioners met at the county seat in Perrysburg and arranged for a survey and new road construction along Hull's route; yet the process of upgrading the road would continue to be complicated by the swampy conditions.

Today, one can travel the majority of Hull's Trace by following modern U.S. 68 from Urbana, Ohio, through gently rolling farmlands and Amish communities and on north through Bellefontaine and Kenton. At Findlay, follow Main Street north to the Village of Van Buren, where Interstate 75 is constructed on top of the trace; continue on I-75 north into the Great Black Swamp region at the village of North Baltimore, exiting the interstate at Cygnet. Here, one will observe some of the flattest terrain in the United States. From Cygnet, Ohio Route 25 follows the same route as the Dixie Highway and Hull's Trace north through Bowling Green, Perrysburg and Maumee. Angling northeast through Toledo, the Dixie Highway roughly follows Hull's Trace to Monroe, Michigan, and terminates in downtown Detroit, across the Detroit River from Windsor, Canada.

The majority of this two-hundred-mile trace has been improved and segments rerouted; however, there is one section of the historic corduroy road still in existence near the historical location of the Wyandotte village of Brownstown, located south of Detroit, at the mouth of the Huron River. The only known remaining 380 meters of the wooden roadbed is listed on the National Register of Historic Places as a significant national treasure of the Greater Detroit metropolitan area. Partially submerged timbers forming the corduroy base of Hull's Trace may be observed by taking Dixie Highway north from Monroe to Rockwood, Michigan, where the route is known locally as West Jefferson Avenue.

PART II

The Settlers

6

Settling the Land

Food Traditions of the Early European Pioneers and Settlers

At the age of thirteen, John Chapman began serving an apprenticeship that his father arranged for him with an orchardist in Leominster, Massachusetts. The orchardist was a man named Mr. Crawford, and he managed apple trees. By the time Chapman turned eighteen in 1792, he had already begun to feel the need to roam, and he had roamed as far west as Ohio. Between the time of his first visit to the Midwest and his second in 1802, Chapman embraced the teachings of Emanuel Swedenborg and became a preacher of Swedenborgianism, or the New Church, and sought to spread Swedenborg's teachings to whoever would listen.

As Chapman wandered from place to place across New York, Pennsylvania, Ohio and Indiana, he taught Swedenborg's form of Christianity to the Native Americans and the European settlers he interacted with and claimed that he was able to convert many of them to the New Church. As part of his worldview, Chapman was opposed to violence of any kind toward both humans and animals, and he was said to have refused the hospitality of the Native Americans' and settlers' campfires in the Ohio and Indiana wilderness because bugs would fly into the flame and be burned alive. Chapman was well known throughout Ohio and Indiana by his eccentricity and the strange garb he usually wore. In the most inclement weather he might be seen barefooted and almost naked, except when he chanced to pick up articles of old clothing. Despite his appearance, the settlers welcomed him to their camps, and from their interactions with Chapman, many started referring to him as Johnny Appleseed.

While he traveled through New York and Pennsylvania, Chapman harvested apple seeds from cider presses and apple nurseries to plant in the Midwest. The seeds Chapman gathered were likely seeds from the most commonly grown variety of the time: the Rambo apple, a greenish yellow apple with dull red stripes that ripens from midsummer to early fall and is noted as a versatile apple. It is said to be good for fresh eating, cooking, baking, drying, cider and apple butter. The Rambo was once widely grown, and in *Varieties of Apples in Ohio*, the "little old-fashioned Rambo" was said to have been found "in almost every old orchard in Ohio and Indiana."

When he would come across a clearing he deemed appropriate for a future apple orchard, Chapman would clear the land and construct fences around the nursery with the brush to prevent his apple nursery from being trampled by animals. He would then plant the seeds and care for the seedlings as they matured. However, cultivating apples using seeds did not guarantee that the apples would be of the same variety or of high quality. This unusual practice of planting trees from seed tends to result in small, poorly flavored apples, so many historians suggest that with very rare exceptions, Chapman's trees would have been best fit for pressing into cider. In an interview with Gwen Ifill of PBS NewsHour, Michael Pollan states that when researching *Botany of Desire*, he "found out that the version of Johnny Appleseed I learned in kindergarten was completely wrong, had been Disney-fied, cleaned up and made very benign. He's a much more interesting character." Pollan goes on to comment about how Chapman was against grafting, and his apples were probably not of an edible variety and could be used only for cider: "Really, what Johnny Appleseed was doing and the reason he was welcome in every cabin in Ohio and Indiana was he was bringing the gift of alcohol to the frontier. He was our American Dionysus."

Johnny Appleseed's greatest contribution to the settlement of the Midwest was not apples used for food but apples used for cider that was then fermented naturally into hard cider. While the apples Chapman and subsequent orchardists planted were an important source of food for the early settlers, many historians agree that John Chapman's greatest contribution to the culinary history and traditions of the regions surrounding the Great Black Swamp was that of introducing alcohol to the Midwest.

Frontier life was often harsh and lonely and filled with hardship. During this period, the alcoholic drinks of choice in America were hard cider and whiskey. While distilling whiskey was a more complex process requiring specialized equipment and training, pressing apples into cider was a relatively inexpensive and easy process that only required access to fresh apples, a cider press and a barrel in which to store the cider. Once the apples were pressed, natural yeasts provided the catalyst for turning sweet cider into hard cider in as little as one to two weeks, depending on the weather. Another alcoholic beverage popular among the early settlers was applejack, or fermented hard cider that went through a rudimentary distilling process for which the cider barrels were left exposed to the cold weather. Whatever ice formed was removed from the cider, which boosted the remaining alcohol content. To add flavor and variation to the applejack, some recipes called for the addition of raisins, sugar or maple syrup.

Many of Indiana's and Ohio's first orchards began with saplings from Chapman's nurseries. His trees fed many of the early white settlers as they struggled to establish farms and homes on the frontier. Chapman eventually developed apple orchards on more than 1,200 acres of land across Pennsylvania, Ohio, Indiana and Illinois. Due to the climate, apples were especially easy to grow and became quite popular in the areas surrounding the Great Black Swamp. And many of the first orchards in Ohio and Indiana began with saplings from Chapman's nurseries.

In his later years, Chapman continued to actively care for his orchards across the Midwest but tended to stay close to the Richland County area of north-central Ohio. He was living with relatives in the Mohican area near Mansfield, Ohio, when he received word that one of his orchards had been damaged, and he set out to care for it. En route, he became ill and died suddenly.

John Chapman passed away near Fort Wayne in Allen County, Indiana, on March 11, 1847. Thereafter, the date of his passing became known locally as Johnny Appleseed Day, and he became commemorated at a variety of apple seed festivals, events and dramas across Indiana and Ohio. A few of the larger, better-known examples are Fort Wayne's Johnny Appleseed Festival, where historical reenacters introduce new generations to the practices of the past; Defiance County, Ohio's AuGlaize Village, which becomes a beehive of activity featuring apple seed–themed crafts and the production of apple butter and sorghum molasses; and near Mifflin, Ohio, the Johnny Appleseed Heritage Center's annual Apple Festival and Johnny Appleseed Outdoor Drama celebrating the life, accomplishments and contributions of John Chapman.

Early on, the Ohio Country was identified with notions of prosperity and bounty, but this was not necessarily the case across the entire northwest quadrant of the state. While the rest of Ohio, Indiana and Michigan were settled much earlier, the Black Swamp region was, at best, a place to cross

Grave site of John Chapman, also known as Johnny Appleseed, on a hill in Fort Wayne, Indiana. *Image courtesy of author.*

through, or around, in order to get to more hospitable lands in other portions of the Northwest Territory. The Great Black Swamp was not an area to settle in. And for many years, the swamp continued to be a significant barrier to western settlement. In order to avoid crossing through the swamp, most settlers heading for Michigan traveled as far as they could by boat on Lake Erie and then by river to reach their desired destination. Likewise, pioneers heading to southern Indiana avoided the swamp altogether by navigating toward their destination via the Ohio River to one of the port cities, such as Evansville. However, settlers bound for northern Indiana and other points beyond, such as Illinois, Wisconsin and Minnesota, still had to contend with the swamp.

The inhospitable conditions created by the geography of the area helped shape the settlement patterns of the region, especially the early growth of urban centers located on the periphery of the swamp, such as Detroit, Findlay, Fort Wayne, Sandusky and Toledo. Of all the major settlements in northwest Ohio, northeast Indiana and southeast Michigan, all are outside the swamp with the exception of Bowling Green, Ohio.

Under water the majority of the year, the densest, swampiest portions of the lands within its boundaries yielded grass that could be cut during the dry season and piled to feed livestock during the winter. As the Wyandotte, Miami, Ottawa and Pottawatomie tribes were gradually pushed out of the areas surrounding the swamp, some minor conflicts occurred over this very practice. Local historians cite an incident in 1832, when Bowling Green's first settler, Elisha Martindale, traveled to the area by means of an old aboriginal trail and claimed forty acres of land surrounding a sand hill near the site of the current Conneaut Elementary School on Haskins Road. The first season he arrived, he camped on the land and was able to cut and stack two ricks of prairie hay to feed his animals. When he returned the following year to build a cabin on his claim, Martindale found his hay burned by the natives. He then set about to carve a living from the land.

Aside from scratching a living from the land, the earliest settlers of the swamp needed to work according to the seasons to improve their land. During the wet season, they drained the land by digging drainage ditches that often led nowhere other than to redirect water away from their cabins and farmland. During winter, they would girdle trees by cutting a six- to eight-inch notch along the entire circumference of the tree. Then in spring, the tree couldn't receive the life-giving sap in the canopy and would die. As trees died, settlers would harvest the wood to cut into lumber and barrel staves and to fire into charcoal to fuel local industries.

As the trees were harvested, a common practice for removing stumps was to light them on fire and let them smolder. While this helped the farmer remove the stumps in only a few seasons, the air the settlers breathed would have been filled with wood smoke all the time. However, an added benefit to the continual, low-hanging pall of wood smoke was that it helped reduce the flying insect population that reproduced in the stagnant waters of the swamp. While the cause was misidentified during the settlement period, malaria was a constant companion for settlers, who thought it was an illness caused by the "miasma," or the unhealthy swamp air, not mosquitos.

As settlers flowed into the more hospitable areas of Ohio, Indiana and Michigan, the early settlers of the Great Black Swamp adopted some of the practices and traditions of the Native Americans by living off the land while slowly draining the swampy land and clearing trees, stumps and undergrowth to plant crops. The culinary practices of the settlers blended the traditions they carried with them and the resources available in the environment they found. Then, they set about to alter their environment to suit their needs.

Tree stumps in a field being cleared near Paulding, Ohio. Paulding County was entirely inside the Great Black Swamp and remains the most sparsely populated county in the region. *Image courtesy of the Center for Archival Collections, Bowling Green State University.*

Eagleville Road in southern Wood County follows the ancient beach moraine of Lake Maumee. The land to the south of the road (right side of the frame) is noticeably ten feet higher than the land to the north side of the road. *Image courtesy of author.*

Over the next few decades, more white settlers gradually entered into the Black Swamp region; however, their settlements were mainly confined to ridges and low sand hills created from glacier deposits. This was the case until shortly before the Civil War broke out in 1860, when a comprehensive drainage was undertaken to drain the Great Black Swamp, greatly increasing the influx of new settlers. The early settlers of this region would learn many of the farming practices introduced to them by the natives they encountered and learn similar hunting and gathering practices. The advantage these early settlers had was that they also used tools and methods common to their former homes in other states or countries.

Numerous settlers also planted orchards from seeds that they brought with them to the region or purchased from people living east of the Appalachian Mountains. Due to the climate, apples and peaches were especially easy to grow and became quite popular. From the apples, early settlers produced apple butter, sweet cider, hard cider, applejack, apple wine and apple moonshine. Moreover, strawberries and Catawba grapes also grew well, and both were used for preserves and winemaking. Depending on their location, settlers also grew many other vegetables, including turnips, cabbage, parsnips, sweet potatoes, yams, onions and leeks.

Most of the original Europeans to settle Ohio raised wheat, corn and other grain crops while adopting the cultivation of the Native American crops of corn, beans and squash. They also introduced the Native Americans to the crops they brought with them, such as watermelon and muskmelon. By 1849, Ohio produced more corn than any other state, and it ranked second in the nation in wheat production. In 1885, the most commonly grown crop was corn, followed by wheat, oats, potatoes, barley, rye and buckwheat. The increase in grain production in the region necessitated the development of mills to grind grain into flour for local and regional use. The surplus was often sold to grain shippers, who would deliver the grain to the nearby shipping ports to be transported to eastern markets and beyond.

Early farmers in the Black Swamp region also raised livestock, most importantly cattle, sheep and pigs. While all of these animals served as food sources for Ohioans, sheep also provided wool that could be sold to the textile factories that opened in Ohio as early as the 1810s. The proceeds from the sale of wool could provide some settlers with enough income to cover their annual operating expenses for the rest of the year. By and large, pigs could be turned loose in the forests to fend for themselves, with an added benefit: as the pigs foraged for food, they also cleared the Great Black Swamp and the surrounding forests of yellow timber rattlesnakes, which the early settlers

Agricultural scene with wheat, wagons and horses at harvest time near Paulding, Ohio, circa 1900. *Image courtesy of the Center for Archival Collections, Bowling Green State University.*

Harvesting grain using a steam-powered reaper in Henry County, Ohio, circa 1900. *Image courtesy of the Wood County Historical Society.*

called "yallers." Pig skin was thick enough to repel the bite of the yellow timber rattler, and the snakes' bite would only anger the pig, which retaliated by eating the snake. What animals they did not either consume or use to breed new herds were sent across the Appalachian Mountains to feed people living in the major cities of the East Coast.

Most of the early farmers who produced a surplus continued to sell their products locally or sent them down the Ohio and Mississippi Rivers to New Orleans. River traffic became even easier with the invention of steamboats. Canals arose during the 1820s and 1830s and diverted some of the traffic from the Ohio River, especially in northern Ohio, where farmers sent their products across Lake Erie to the Erie Canal. The Erie Canal ended at the Hudson River in eastern New York and provided a quick route to East Coast cities.

During the early settlement period, fish—such as walleye, white perch, blue gills, bullheads, crappies, catfish and white bass—were plentiful in the many lakes, rivers and streams, as they had been during the time of the Native Americans in the Great Black Swamp. Game was still hunted for meat and hides. Like the Native Americans who came before them, in the fall and winter, the settlers hunted white-tailed deer and black bear and trapped smaller game such as groundhog, turkey, muskrat, raccoon and turtle. Same as they were for the natives, black bears were highly prized by the settlers for their skins as well as their meat and grease.

A narrative published in 1910 in *The Pioneer Scrap-Book of Wood County and the Maumee Valley* recounts the story of an 1854 bear hunt in which William E. Carothers and Jim Rowland captured and killed two black bears over the first three days of their hunt before witnessing a battle between a bear and their dogs that they would never forget. The men had wounded a four-hundred-pound bear, and the dogs were close on the trail. By the time the men caught up, the dogs had the wounded bear up a partially downed tree and surrounded. As the dogs nipped and harassed the bear, trying to pull it from the tree, it would swing and growl at the dogs. Carothers relates that "the dogs would either pull the bear off the log or cause him to jump from it, when they would all attack him and the snow would fly in clouds. The fierce growls and groans of the rage of the bear could be heard above the din raised by the dogs, which was deafening."

When the bear managed to break free from its attackers, it was soon trapped on another log. Rowland got another shot off, hoping to kill the bear, and then as Rowland was reloading, the men heard "one of the dogs giving a terrible cry of distress and saw the shaggy, black beast standing on his hind legs, with one of the best dogs in his deadly embrace, while with one paw he was beating and crippling the dogs with frightful ferocity." At this point, Carothers delivered the killing shot to the head of the bear. But the kill was hard won, and the chase had covered more than two hundred miles in the Great Black Swamp over four days.

Due to the emotional and physical stress both men endured, it would prove to be the last bear hunt for Carothers and the end of Rowland's entire hunting career. Carothers explains that Rowland "told me years after that he never got over the effects of that chase—that it was more than flesh and bone could endure."

Throughout the various seasons of the year, the early settlers went about gathering mushrooms (such as morels and hen-of-the-woods), black cherries, red mulberry, buckeye nuts, butternuts (white walnut), hickory nuts, black walnuts, American filberts or hazelnuts, acorns, persimmons, honey and sap from maple trees to evaporate into syrup or sugar. The settlers brought with them improved methods and equipment for gathering and evaporating maple sap into syrup or sugar. Like the natives had taught them, the settlers would drill a hole in the tree and insert a wooden spile, from which a wooden

Maple syrup was an important agricultural product for Native Americans and early settlers. Foraged maple sap was evaporated into syrup in sugar shacks like this one. Pictured are Paul Snavely, Gaylord Snavely and Shorty, the dog, at the Henry Bowerman/Snavely Sugar Shack in 1963. This sugar shack was built in 1864 and remained in use for 118 years. *Image courtesy of Paul and Evelyn Snavely.*

When the original 1864 sugar shack became unusable, it was replaced. The current Snavely Sugar Shack in Republic, Ohio, was built in 1982 on the site of the former Henry Bowerman/Snavely Sugar Shack. *Image courtesy of author.*

gathering pail was hung. The settlers would then collect the sap and evaporate it down in a cast-iron or copper kettle over an open fire, which allowed for more control and consistency of the final product. For many early settlers, maple syrup and maple sugar were the only means of sweetening their food available to them, and making sugar was one of their most important mid- to late-winter activities. What's more, access to standing groves of sugar maple trees "served as one of the many incentives for white settlement in the upper Great Lakes region," according to Keller in "America's Native Sweet."

Buttermilk Biscuits

2¼ cups self-rising flour
½ teaspoon salt
¾ cup shortening
I cup buttermilk

Combine dry ingredients and mix in shortening with a pastry cutter (the faster the better—you don't want the fats to melt). When mixture reaches mealy texture, add buttermilk and mix until just combined. Pour out on floured wax paper. Pat the dough out with your hands until dough is not sticky (add a little flour if necessary). Fold double. Cut biscuits with a biscuit cutter.
Bake on a cookie sheet at 425 degrees Fahrenheit (220 degrees Celsius) for 20 to 25 minutes. Yields 6 to 12 biscuits, depending on desired thickness of dough and size of biscuit cutter.

———◆◆◆———

Apple Butter for a Crowd
Historical Society of Grand Rapids, Ohio

50 gallons apple cider, pressed from around 38 bushels mixed apples
15 bushels mixed apples (Courtland, Jonathan, Empire and Yellow Delicious are best. Do not use Red Delicious.)
75 pounds sugar

Day One: Procure a 50-gallon copper kettle, 38 bushels of mixed apples (a variety of ⅓ sweet apples, ⅓ tart apples and ⅓ juicy apples works best) and a cider press to press 50 gallons of apple cider. Stoke a fire and set up the kettle over the flames. Be sure to have an ample supply of firewood as the

next process will take an entire day. Boil 50 gallons of cider down to about 10 gallons of thick syrup, or "liquor." Reserve for day three.
Day Two: Peel and core around 15 bushels of apples, cover and reserve for day three.
Day Three: Bring the apple liquor back to a boil and add apples to the kettle. Stir with a long-handled stirring stick that has dried cornhusks wrapped around the paddle. Keep stirring the apple butter constantly so it does not burn and taint the flavor of the entire batch. Add more apples as the mixture cooks down. Cook continuously at full boil for around six hours, until smooth. Somewhere around hour six, check the apple butter for consistency. Do this by dipping some out and putting it on a slightly tilted plate while looking for the "run" or the "weep" to go away. Once the butter reaches your desired consistency, add sugar and stir until the sugar is dissolved and apple butter is back to a full boil. Remove from fire. Fill jars immediately. Makes 330 pints.

CROCKPOT APPLE BUTTER
Historical Society of Grand Rapids, Ohio

About 16 large apples—enough to fill a 4-quart crockpot to about 1½ inches from top when quartered. (Apples should be from a mix of varieties: Courtland, Jonathan, Empire and Yellow Delicious are best. Do not use Red Delicious.)
4 teaspoons cinnamon
½ teaspoon cloves
½ teaspoon salt
3 cups sugar
4 tablespoons water

Peel, core and quarter apples. Combine cinnamon, cloves, salt and sugar in a medium-sized bowl. Toss with apples in a large bowl (or in multiple batches) and then add spiced apples to crockpot. Add water and set on high. When hot, turn crockpot to low and cook all day. When apples are fully cooked down, put small amounts in food processor and pulse quickly until smooth. Makes 8 pints. If canning the apple butter, put the mixture in jars and seal while still hot.

CORN BREAD
Grand Rapids Applebutter Festival

1 cup cornmeal
1 cup flour
1 tablespoon baking powder
½ teaspoon salt
2 to 4 tablespoons sugar
1 egg
1 cup milk
¼ cup melted lard, butter or oil

Mix cornmeal, flour, baking powder, salt and sugar. Set aside. Beat egg and then add milk and lard, butter or oil. Add liquids to cornmeal mixture and stir just enough to mix. Fill greased 8- by 8-inch pan half full. Bake at 425 degrees for 20 to 25 minutes until lightly brown. Serves 4.

CORN PUDDING

¾ cup milk
1 (17-ounce) can whole kernel corn, drained
1 (16.5-ounce) can cream-style corn
1¼ cups crushed rich, butter-flavored crackers, divided
2 tablespoons chopped onion
2 eggs, lightly beaten
2 teaspoons sugar
½ teaspoon salt
⅛ teaspoon pepper
1 tablespoon butter or margarine, melted
⅛ teaspoon ground nutmeg

Preheat oven to 350 degrees. In large saucepan, heat milk but do not boil; remove from heat. Stir in both cans of corn, 1 cup crushed crackers, onion, eggs, sugar, salt and pepper. Pour into lightly greased 1½-quart baking dish. In small bowl combine remaining crushed crackers, butter and nutmeg. Sprinkle on top of corn mixture. Bake 30 to 35 minutes, or until set. Serves 8.

PIONEER CHICKEN AND NOODLES
Doug Kaufman

1 pound cooked boneless, skinless chicken breasts, torn into large pieces
9 cups hot water
¾ cup chopped carrot
¾ cup chopped celery
1 cup chopped onion
1 ½ tablespoons chicken bouillon (or soup base)
¾ cup butter, melted
½ teaspoon black pepper
½ teaspoon salt
1 pound homemade noodles (recipe follows)

In a large stockpot, mix chicken pieces, water, carrot, celery, onion, chicken bouillon, melted butter, pepper and salt. Bring to a boil and turn to low heat to simmer for 30 minutes. Add noodles and simmer on medium-low heat for an additional 10 minutes, or until noodles are tender. Serves 4 to 6.
For northwest Ohio–style chicken potpie, serve chicken and noodles over mashed potatoes with a roll and a side of corn or green beans.

NOODLES

3 egg yolks
1 whole egg
1 teaspoon salt
3 tablespoons cold water
2 cups flour

Beat the egg yolks with the whole egg until very light. Beat in the salt and water. Stir in the flour and work with hands until blended. Divide dough into two parts. Roll out each part as thin as possible (¼ inch to ⅛ inch thick) on a lightly floured board. Let stand until partially dry (like chamois skin), at least 1 hour. Then roll up like a jellyroll and cut into strips of any desired width. Shake out strips and allow them to finish drying before using or storing them.

Dumplings for Soup

2 cups flour
4 teaspoons baking powder
1 teaspoon salt
4 tablespoons oil or softened butter
¾ cup milk

Sift flour, baking powder and salt into a bowl. Add oil or butter and cut with a pastry blender or knife until mix is crumbly. Add just enough milk to make a stiff batter—do not over mix. In a mixing bowl, combine dumpling ingredients and mix well to form a stiff dough. Drop by tablespoonfuls into simmering soup. Cover and simmer for 15 to 20 minutes. Serve immediately. Serves 4 to 6.

Tomato Pudding
Bountiful Ohio Cookbook

4 cups cubed bread (about 8 slices)
½ cup butter or margarine, melted
1 (15-ounce) can tomato puree
½ to 1 cup firmly packed light brown sugar
1 tablespoon lemon juice
½ teaspoon salt
⅛ teaspoon pepper

Preheat oven to 350 degrees. Arrange bread in a lightly greased 1-quart baking dish; pour butter over bread. In a medium saucepan, combine remaining ingredients and bring to a boil. Reduce heat, cover and simmer for 5 minutes. Pour over bread cubes; do not stir. Bake 35 to 40 minutes, or until top is puffed and dark brown. Serves 8.

7

Altering the Landscape

An Era of Canal Networks and Drainage Systems

During the late 1700s and early 1800s the majority of goods transportation in and out of the Midwest was done by way of water, and the most prosperous settlements developed early on as trading and shipping hubs. What's more, these settlements were ideally situated to draw from the surrounding region for their support. As the surrounding regions developed, products and crops from the tri-state area of Indiana, Michigan and Ohio were transported by wagon to ports on rivers and the Great Lakes and then sent by boat on the network of lakes and rivers in the region to be sold at markets in more populous areas of the East. The most common boats used for transportation of people and goods during the late eighteenth and early nineteenth centuries were flatboats. The first steamboat arrived on the Ohio River in 1811, and within thirty years, there were literally hundreds of steamboats on the Mississippi and Ohio Rivers. Steamboats were also used to ship grain and other goods on the Great Lakes.

To facilitate the transportation of Ohio grain to the East, as early as the late 1810s, Governors Thomas Worthington and Ethan Allen Brown of Ohio supported internal improvements that would bring greater prosperity to the people of the state. This was in the form of a canal-based transportation network intended to link Lake Erie with the Ohio River. In Ohio, three corridors were originally planned, one descending the eastern length of the state, one down the central area of the state and a third running from the mouth of the Maumee, near present-day Toledo, south through Dayton to Cincinnati. After a series of failed starts and setbacks, work began on a

Piliod Mill, on the Miami and Erie Canal, in Providence (Grand Rapids), Ohio. In 1886, Augustine Pilliod bought and modernized the existing sawmill and gristmill, Manor Mill, constructed in 1822 by Peter Manor. Renamed and donated to the Providence Metropark District in 1974, the Isaac Ludwig Mill is an authentic, functioning, turn-of-the-century grist- and flour mill. It also has a turbine-powered, functioning sawmill. *Image courtesy of the Wood County Historical Society.*

hybrid of the eastern and central network of canals on July 4, 1825. Work began on what would become known as the Miami and Erie Canal on July 21 of that same year.

The canal era would prove to be one of the major events contributing to the opening up of the swamp for settlement for many reasons, transportation being only one. Because the massive public work brought such an influx of workers for the construction of the canal, there was also a need for industries that provided support for the workers. Construction of the Miami and Erie Canal and the Wabash and Erie Canal required a significant amount of human labor, and the canal companies advertised in foreign presses for immigrant labor. The majority of the laborers attracted to the work of building the Ohio canal networks came from Ireland and Germany, where economic conditions were so poor that a new life as a laborer was promising.

By 1833, the Ohio and Erie Canal, linking Cleveland on Lake Erie with Portsmouth on the Ohio River, was complete. The Miami and Erie Canal, linking Toledo on Lake Erie with Cincinnati on the Ohio River, would take an additional twelve years to finish. This was because the state legislature originally authorized its completion from Cincinnati to only just north of Dayton. In 1830, the Ohio legislature earmarked funds for the Miami and Erie Canal's extension to Defiance and Lake Erie. Additional feeder canals were built to expand the network. Of these feeder canals, the most important to Indiana was the Wabash and Erie Canal, which joined the Miami and Erie Canal south of Defiance, Ohio, at Canal Junction. From the junction, the Wabash and Erie Canal followed the Maumee River to Fort Wayne. Then, the route followed the Wabash River to Terre Haute and terminated at the Ohio River at the port of Evansville, Indiana.

Some of the laborers who had signed on to build the canal network remained to claim land inside the swamp as a portion of their wages after completing the project. While the Irish laborers tended to move on to other parts of the United States, immigrants of German descent tended to claim land in the swamp and were joined later by their families. Some of these German families settled down and remained on the same farms for generations, and there is still evidence of the pride in these intergenerational ties displayed on barns indicating the family name and the date of the farm's establishment, some from as far back as the 1820s.

While some of the early immigrants were attracted by the promise of jobs working on the canals, others were attracted by the promise of inexpensive farmland. Unscrupulous land developers advertised inexpensive farmland to people in Germany by promoting images of vast acreage of fertile land waiting for the plow. The reality was that much of the land these settlers bought was some of the thickest and densest forest and swampland American settlers had ever encountered. Selling everything they had, many of these German immigrants bought plots of land, sight unseen, and boarded ships to travel to America to claim it. Upon arriving, they set about the task of transforming the physical landscape into the idyllic one they had been sold. This was no easy task. One pioneer account describes the swamp as an "impenetrable mass: great trees and dense undergrowth, stagnant waters, deep mud, dangerous animals and a multitude of pesty insects." While some land was settled by these German immigrants, when they contemplated further settlement, they "were laughed at for their credulity if they insisted it would be a habitable region." Even with the completion of the Miami and Erie Canal and the Wabash and Erie Canal, the Black Swamp region would remain sparsely populated until after the American Civil War.

In 1851, David and Kezia Kohl bought land for two dollars an acre in Perrysburg and settled in the Great Black Swamp. By their account, at that time, water covered all but the high ground, and the woods were so dense that their children were not allowed to go far from the home for fear of getting lost. Parents felled trees so their children could walk to school on top of the logs. All across the Black Swamp region, early European settlers who moved there had to clear native ash, beech, maple, oak, black walnut, chestnut and sycamore trees before they could plant their first crops. Clearing land for farming involved pulling up the smallest trees and roots, cutting down and burning medium-sized trees and girdling—or cutting a groove in the tree trunk so that it would eventually die and fall over—large trees. Settlers used some of the logs to build their homes. Over time, the land was cleared of trees, but drainage remained a problem.

The early settlers drained the land by digging open ditches two to three feet deep and three feet wide at the top. These ditches often led nowhere; however, the purpose of these ditches was to provide a place where water could drain and leave the surrounding ground to be farmed. There are accounts of early settlers in the swamp who dug ditches underneath the floorboards of their cabins that served dual purposes: first, to drain the water from around their home; second, to provide a source of water for cooking, drinking and bathing. All the settlers needed to do was install a door in the floorboards that could be opened up, and water could be gathered from the drainage ditch. Unfortunately for the settlers, these open ditches attracted bugs and mosquitoes that added to their hardships. To counteract the effects of the increased bug population, settlers would have smudge fires burning day and night from spring through autumn, and the air would be heavy with smoke.

To help combat the problems created by standing water in open ditches, the settlers began to construct drains made by nailing together slabs of wood in an inverted V and then laying the slabs in the bottom of their trenches. It was after the end of the Civil War when German immigrants realized that the key to taming the Great Black Swamp was held in the swamp itself. More precisely, the key to draining the Great Black Swamp was the deposits of clay in the swamp that could be quarried, shaped and baked into drainage tiles that could then be laid in covered trenches leading to drainage ditches that would sluice the waters of the swamp into the streams and rivers that

flow into Lake Erie. In 1859, a law was passed providing for a system of public ditches to drain the land. By 1870, the swamp was still only half cleared. The settlers didn't have surveying instruments to help them lay out the network of clay drainage tiles and drainage ditches, so they mainly worked during the wet season to gauge the fall of the land. During the summer, when the higher land dried out, they carried buckets of water with them to judge the slope.

Eventually, after a period of intense lumbering and draining, the swamp had nearly vanished, and the area became a major agricultural region. As the landscape was increasingly altered toward the end of the nineteenth century, the swamp gave way to some of the most fertile land in the entire nation. What took nature tens of thousands of years to form was drained and planted with crops within fifty years. The only reminders of the Great Black Swamp left are the remains of the drainage ditches dug to drain it.

Eventually, the canal system fell out of use, and the goods that were previously transported either to the Great Lakes port at Toledo or to the Ohio River port at Evansville and Cincinnati were shipped via rail and eventually overland on the series of highways that cross the state north to south and east to west. The Lincoln Highway, America's first transcontinental highway, was conceived in 1913 and connected northern Indiana and Ohio with Times Square in New York City and Lincoln Park in San Francisco, California. While the Lincoln Highway was eventually renamed Route 30, much of the highway is still in use today. Another east–west corridor was built between 1949 and 1955—the Ohio Turnpike and Indiana Toll Road. It is part of the modern interstate highway system and signed as I-80, I-90 and I-76 in Ohio. From north to south, the Dixie Highway was constructed and expanded between 1915 and 1927 and linked Ontario, Canada, to Florida City, Florida. Portions

Top: Men sawing logs at the W.G. Dangler Tile Mill and Saw Mill in 1895. Village of Paulding, Paulding County, Ohio. *Image courtesy of the Center for Archival Collections, Bowling Green State University.*

Left: Men pose with clay drainage tiles and a whiskey jug stopped with a corn cob at the Broughton Tile Mill in Broughton, Ohio, in 1904. The key to draining the Great Black Swamp lay in its own clay soil, excavated and baked into drainage tiles. *Image courtesy of the Center for Archival Collections, Bowling Green State University.*

A family moving north to Michigan stops on Hull's Trace (North Main Street in Bowling Green) to pose for a photograph, circa 1900. Note the Wood County Courthouse in the center distance. *Image courtesy of the Wood County Historical Society.*

Above: Between 1915 and 1927, Hull's Trace was upgraded with a macadamized (crushed-stone) surface as part of the Dixie Highway, a modernized north–south route from Florida to Detroit, Michigan, and then on to Windsor, Ontario, Canada. *Image courtesy of the Wood County Historical Society.*

Opposite, bottom: Hull's Trace in North Baltimore, circa 1900, locally known as Findlay-Perrysburg Mud Pike, remained a difficult road to travel well into the twentieth century. *Image courtesy of the Wood County Historical Society.*

of the highway still are in use, but it has been replaced by Interstate 75, which runs north from the southern tip of Florida through Cincinnati to Toledo and on to the Ontario, Canada border. Even with the decline of the canal system, the Great Black Swamp region remained an important intersection for transportation and commerce.

8

Making the Land Their Own

German Americans

The reality of a region dominated by a vast swamp provided opportunities for immigrants, who had little more than manpower, to start draining the swamp and carve an existence out of this densely forested, swampy area. As mentioned previously, white settlement into what would become the tri-state area of northeast Indiana, southeast Michigan and northwest Ohio was slowly achieved in stages, while the Native American population was gradually forced out. The inhospitable terrain slowed immigration to the area, which in turn attracted a more ethnically diverse population of late immigrants. Of all the immigrant groups that would eventually call the Black Swamp home, the Germans would be the first and the largest group of settlers in the area.

To better understand the German immigration into the Great Black Swamp, it is necessary to view it in the context of the forces driving German immigration to America in general. While the first permanent German settlement in the American colonies was founded at Germantown, Pennsylvania, in 1683, the first German settlers in America had arrived in Virginia at the time of the founding of Jamestown Colony in 1607. Since none of the historical German states had overseas colonies, it was not until the 1680s that significant groups of German immigrants arrived in the British colonies. These early German Americans settled primarily in upstate New York and Pennsylvania. Among them were the Amish and Mennonites, who became known as the Pennsylvania Dutch (Deutsch). Many were highly skilled laborers, craftsmen and farmers who were being pushed out of Europe by shortages of land and religious or political oppression. Some arrived seeking the opportunity to own land and have religious or political freedom, others for economic opportunities greater than those in Europe and still others simply for the chance to start fresh in the New World.

The greatest number of German immigrants arrived between 1820 and the start of World War I, during which time nearly 6 million Germans immigrated to the United States. Of those arriving before 1850, most were farmers who could not purchase land in Germany due to laws used to maintain undivided property. They sought productive land where their intensive farming techniques and advanced methods of animal husbandry would pay off. The German Revolutions of 1848 brought a wave of political refugees who became known as Forty-Eighters. And after 1850, many of the skilled professionals came to cities where German-speaking districts soon emerged, such as the Over-the-Rhine neighborhood in Cincinnati and the German Village in Columbus, Ohio. Immigration continued in very large numbers during the nineteenth century, with some 8 million arrivals from Germany.

During this period of intensive German immigration, about 250,000 German Jews arrived in the United States, and by the 1870s, they had sponsored reform synagogues in many small cities across the country. In total, about 2 million Eastern European Jews arrived from the 1880s to 1924, bringing more traditional religious practices. In the Black Swamp region, the majority of these German Jews settled in larger cities such as Fort Wayne and Toledo; Toledo still has one of the largest Jewish communities in Ohio, with congregations dating back to 1867. There are also Jewish communities in Fremont, Bowling Green and Findlay.

German Americans immigrated to the midwestern states of Ohio and Indiana for many of the same reasons that brought German immigrants to the United States in general. For many, the urban centers of Cleveland, Columbus, Cincinnati, Toledo, Indianapolis and Fort Wayne served as jumping off points where immigrants would settle for a time in the various ethnic neighborhoods and build up the resources needed to acquire land for farming in the more rural areas.

Enticed by the pastoral descriptions of rich, fertile farmland promoted by the Miami and Erie and Wabash and Erie Canal companies—which had large tracts of land to sell for low prices—many German settlers purchased unseen land inside the Great Black Swamp. One historical narrative describes a German family who bought forty acres of swampland in Ohio's Henry County and, upon arrival, were surprised to see the that the land was covered with primeval forest. While the wife wept for their bad decision, the husband set about felling the trees, clearing the land of stumps and draining the swampy ground into a nearby creek. It took the family ten years to clear the farm, but they turned the former swamp into highly productive farmland and made enough off their crops to acquire more land and expand.

During this time, German American culture flourished in these urban areas, and some of the contributions Germans made to American culture include holiday traditions, such as Christmas trees and Easter bunnies that lay eggs. In terms of cuisine, the German Americans developed breweries and wineries and introduced their neighbors to hearty sausages and specialty meats.

Perhaps the greatest contribution of German Americans to American culture and culinary history was the introduction of the German practices of fermenting wine and brewing beer. As mentioned previously, before the German brewers introduced beer and German-style wine to America, the alcoholic drinks of choice were hard cider and whiskey.

From the 1840s into the 1920s, evangelical Protestant churches, the Woman's Christian Temperance Union and the Anti-Saloon League used pressure politics to achieve their goal of nationwide Prohibition. Emphasizing the need to reduce domestic violence in the home, the temperance movement sought to destroy what it saw as political corruption rampant in the saloons and to break the political power of the German-based brewing industry. In short, Prohibition was motivated in part by popular anti-German sentiment of the day.

Despite reoccurring waves of anti-German sentiment during the late nineteenth and early twentieth centuries, the Germans worked hard to maintain and cultivate their culture and language, especially through newspapers and classes in elementary and high schools. According to historian Walter Kamphoefner, a "number of big cities introduced German into their public school programs." For example, Indianapolis, Cincinnati and Cleveland "had what we now call two-way immersion programs: school taught half in German, half in English." This was a tradition that continued "all the way down to World War I." The common practice of using German in municipal and cultural institutions and to transact business may have been one of the contributing factors of the anti-German sentiment that festered during World War I, which brought the most serious challenge to their identity. By the end of World War II, the German language, which had always been commonly used instead of English for public and official matters across the Midwest, was in serious decline and would soon disappear altogether.

Residents at the Wood County Home, snapping green beans, circa 1940. *Image courtesy of the Wood County Historical Society.*

Produce pavilion at the 1888 Ohio State Fair promoting the varieties of produce grown and glass manufactured in Bowling Green, Ohio. *Image courtesy of the Wood County Historical Society.*

While the loss of the German language in the United States was devastating for the German American population, German Americans continued to hold onto many of their cultural institutions while substituting English for German. Additionally, they continued to prepare and eat the same foods they had prepared and eaten previously and continued to honor their German ancestry and heritage. At the time of the 2010 U.S. census, 17 percent of all Americans claimed total or partial German ancestry, which makes German the country's largest self-reported ancestral group.

By percentage in the 2010 census, North Dakota has the largest concentration of German Americans with 46.8 percent of the population claiming German ancestry. Also by percentage, Ohio has the eighth-largest population of German Americans with 26.5 percent of residents claiming German ancestry. Indiana is the thirteenth with 22.7 percent, and Michigan is the sixteenth with 22.3 percent of its population reporting German ancestry. However, when one looks at the sheer number of German Americans living in these states, Ohio has the third-largest German American population in the United States with 3,231,788; Michigan has the seventh-largest population at 2,271,090; and Indiana has the eleventh-largest population with 1,629,766 German Americans. By contrast, California has the largest German American population in the nation with 5,517,470; Pennsylvania has the second-largest German American population in the nation with 3,491,269; and North Dakota comes in at thirty-ninth largest in terms of German Americans with only 290,452.

The German settlers grew vegetables to pickle and cabbage to ferment into sauerkraut. They preserved eggs by pickling them and prepared hearty stick-to-your-bones meals that were heavy with starches and carbs like chicken or beef noodles ladled over mashed potatoes and served with bread. During the winter, they would enjoy German potato pancakes served with applesauce or sour cream and hot German potato salad prepared with onion and bacon drippings. They also prepared many dishes with smoked pork and sauerkraut, such as smoked pork chops and sauerkraut, smoked sausage and sauerkraut and noodle casseroles prepared with sausage and sauerkraut. Other popular dishes that were commonly associated with the German settlers were creamy salads and chicken soups with homemade noodles, spaetzle or dumplings. There were also snipple bean and rivel soups and sweets, such as apple dumplings, lebkuchen, springerle and Amish sugar cookies.

To the wilderness of the Black Swamp, they brought their sausage-making traditions, most identifiable in the form of bratwurst. The region has its own characteristic sausages made from locally grown and harvested

Snipple bean soup prepared by the Pemberville Historical Society for one of the many community celebrations it hosts or participates in. *Image courtesy of author.*

Shirley Pickering preparing rivel soup in her home kitchen in Deshler, Ohio. *Image courtesy of author.*

Sauerkraut, beef and noodles and a bratwurst sandwich (clockwise around the plate) are foods commonly presented at German American festivals and hometown festivals across the region. *Image courtesy of author.*

An unnamed meat market, probably in North Baltimore, Ohio, circa 1900. *Image courtesy of the Wood County Historical Society.*

meats. Sausage-making traditions across this area tend to lean toward a southern German or Bavarian style of production in which ground beef, pork or venison is blended with spices and other inclusions to produce fresh, smoked, dry or bulk sausages, with or without natural or artificial casing. German-style sausages produced in the region include bratwurst, knackwurst, summer sausage, landjagers, wieners or frankfurters, bologna, breakfast-style bulk sausage and the whole-hog sausage patty, known locally as a Pork-A-Lean.

While businesses come and go, ethnic traditions in this area tend to remain static. To evidence this, there are butcher shops—such as Belleville Brothers in Bowling Green; Jacob's Meats and Fort Defiance Meats in Defiance; Tanks Meats in Elmore; Jamison Meats, Hill's, Tom Didier and Albright's Meats in Fort Wayne; Herm's Fresh Meat in Napoleon; Belleville's in North Baltimore; Frobose Custom Meats in Pemberville; and House of Meats in Toledo—that continue to offer sausages and specialty meats prepared using closely guarded German-style traditional recipes presented alongside new sausage and specialty meat products intended to suit changing tastes. Two examples of changing tastes in sausage would be German-style butcher shops preparing Polish-style kielbasa and French- or Cajun-style andouille.

GRANDMA JEREW'S GERMAN CASSEROLE
Kandice Springer

2 pounds bulk bratwurst
1 small onion, chopped
1 (8-ounce) package extra thin noodles, such as Inn Maid brand
1 (16-ounce) jar sauerkraut, drained
½ teaspoon pepper
1 teaspoon sugar

Fry bratwurst and onion. Cook noodles and drain. Combine everything in a large bowl and then pour into a 13- by 9- by 2-inch pan. Bake at 325 degrees for 30 minutes. Sausage can be substituted for bratwurst. Serves 6 to 8.
Note: This casserole has been sold at the First United Methodist Bratwurst Festival since 1983. *From* Food for My Household, *First United Methodist Church, Bucyrus, Ohio.*

Sauerkraut directly translated means "sour cabbage" and is finely cut cabbage that has been salted and fermented. It has a long shelf life and a distinctive sour flavor. It's a hearty food often associated with the German population in America, but German Americans are not the only ethnic group that eats sauerkraut. It is also commonly eaten by Russians, Polish and Irish. Among many families of German descent, the combination of sauerkraut and pork is eaten on New Year's Day as a way to welcome the New Year and to bring the family good luck.

Cabbage, the main ingredient in sauerkraut, has been an important crop for the German Americans living in the Black Swamp for generations. Cabbage is a hearty foodstuff that does well in the cold and can be stored for long periods without significant maintenance. Across the region, cabbage growers and sauerkraut makers support many families who work either year-round or seasonally in the industry. Some of the largest producers are located on the eastern side of the Black Swamp in Pemberville and Fremont, Ohio. The Fremont Company of Fremont, Ohio, has been in business since 1905 and is the maker of Frank's and Snow Floss Kraut. Hirzel Farms in Pemberville, Ohio, is a fifth-generation family farm that manages more than two thousand acres of land, seven hundred of which are certified organic. They are the producers of Silverfleece Sauerkraut and Dei Fratelli tomato product lines.

SLOW COOKER SAUERKRAUT AND SAUSAGE
Connie Ehlers

1 package Echrich sausage (kielbasa, smoked turkey or beef)
1 (32-ounce) jar sauerkraut
1 small onion
2 tablespoons brown sugar
1 tablespoon caraway seeds

In medium bowl, combine sauerkraut, diced onion, brown sugar and caraway seeds and then place in slow cooker. Slice sausage into small pieces and arrange over the sauerkraut. Cook on high for two hours, stirring occasionally, and then reduce to low setting and cook for two more hours. Serve with mashed potatoes.

Community and family gatherings among the German American population living in the Black Swamp region would not be the same without their iconic dishes, and perhaps one of the most iconic dishes after bratwurst and sauerkraut would be German potato salad. It is a popular menu choice of cooks preparing food for a large number of people because it is easily made in large quantities, can be prepared in advance and refrigerated until needed and requires inexpensive ingredients. Typically served at festivals, picnics, outdoor barbecues and potlucks, German potato salad is often presented as a side dish paired with smoked pork, sausage, bratwurst or grilled pork chops. The recipe below is a staple at the Christmas party potluck at the Women's Club in Deshler, Ohio. To feed a large crowd, prepare it according to the roaster instructions in Connie Ehlers's recipe.

GERMAN POTATO SALAD
Connie Ehlers

16 cold potatoes, cooked and cubed
¼ cup parsley flakes
16 slices bacon, cooked and crumbled
6 tablespoons flour
⅔ cup diced onion
6 tablespoons bacon grease
1⅓ cups water
2 cups sugar
2 tablespoons salt
⅔ cup vinegar

Place potatoes, parsley and crumbled bacon in dish. Place flour and onion in the leftover bacon grease. Add remaining ingredients, stirring constantly. Cook until bubbly and thickened. Pour over potatoes, parsley and bacon. Can heat in oven or serve cold. Serves 8 to 10.

To fill a roaster, substitute these portions and follow the preparation directions above:

25 pounds potatoes
6 pounds bacon
4 batches of sauce

The German American population is also made more identifiable by its love of creamy salads. Traditionally, dairy products were most commonly consumed during the spring and early summer while the cows were having calves and raising them. During this time, cheeses were produced to preserve the protein-rich milk for other times of the year when milk wasn't available.

A family picnic in Bowling Green, Ohio, circa 1910. *Image courtesy of Tom McLaughlin Sr.*

Also during this time of the year, cream was gathered and used to make sour cream—which formed the base of many recipes.

When cream wasn't available, an appropriate substitute for the desired creamy texture in a dish was mayonnaise. Mayonnaise is a stable emulsion of oil, egg yolk and either vinegar or lemon juice. There are many ingredients that may be added for additional variety. While the origins of mayonnaise are disputed, commercial mayonnaise has been available in the United States since the early twentieth century, and many German dishes use mayonnaise or other sauces with mayonnaise as a base. For example, ranch dressing is made of buttermilk or sour cream, mayonnaise and minced green onions, along with other seasonings, and is commonly consumed across the Black Swamp region and the entire Midwest.

One salad that combines fresh vegetables and a creamy dressing is pea salad. Pea salad is typically served cold and presented along with other salads at a salad bar. It is a popular side dish at both Amish and "home-style" restaurants across the region. The following recipe for pea salad was provided to me by one of the chefs at an Amish restaurant called Essen House located in the tiny village of Antwerp, located on both the Maumee River and the former Wabash and Erie Canal on the border of Ohio and Indiana.

PEA SALAD
Debbie Sigman

1 cup celery, chopped
1 cup chopped white or yellow onions
1 cup chopped carrots
1 cup frozen peas, defrosted and drained
1 fresh lemon
1 cup Mexican blend cheese
½ cup bacon crumbles
3 hard-boiled eggs, sliced
1 cup mayonnaise (not salad dressing)

Place celery, onion, carrot and peas in a large bowl. Squeeze the lemon juice over top and toss all together. Add cheese, bacon and egg and then add mayonnaise to desired consistency. Toss gently and serve. Serves 6 to 8.

Also commonly presented at salad bars in both "home-style" and Amish restaurants in the Black Swamp region are pickled eggs. The following recipes do not have their origins as restaurant food but as home-style food for the German American, Amish and Mennonite populations that settled in the Black Swamp. Pickling eggs made it possible to carry eggs on long journeys or out to the field for a midday snack. Today, they are a common food presented in restaurants playing up to local identity, appealing to locals who want a taste of home or tourists seeking a taste of place and heritage.

PICKLED BEET EGGS

2 cups canned beet juice
¾ cups sugar
1 tablespoon allspice to taste
1 dozen shelled boiled eggs

Bring first three ingredients to a boil. Once cooled, combine eggs and liquid in container and refrigerate overnight.

Pickled Mustard Eggs

1 dozen eggs
4 tablespoons yellow mustard
⅔ cup sugar
½ teaspoon salt
¾ cup white vinegar
¾ cup water
2 drops yellow food coloring

Boil and peel eggs and put into a heat-proof container.
Mix remaining ingredients in a saucepan and bring to a boil, stirring almost constantly. Pour sauce over eggs. Let cool. Put container in refrigerator for 72 hours to let eggs absorb the sauce.

In this part of the nation, chicken potpie is not a thick chicken gravy with chicken and vegetables baked in a savory two-layered pastry crust. It's a plate of creamy mashed potatoes with chicken and noodles ladled over the top. It's a hearty and inexpensive food for hardworking people. Many dishes here in the Black Swamp region use this preparation method of stacking starches to prepare carbohydrate-heavy, stick-to-your-ribs meals. This dish may be one of the oldest in the region and can be traced back anecdotally to the early settlers who needed to prepare tasty and filling meals with what they could procure from their environment. Instead of being a "left-over" dish, chicken and noodles was often considered to be a "planned-over" dish, for which the carcass and leftovers of a Sunday dinner of roasted chicken could be made into a second meal by turning it into stock, pairing it with vegetables and adding homemade noodles before ladling all of it over mashed potatoes. The following recipe for homemade chicken and noodles has been updated to use modern ingredients. I have also included a recipe provided to me by the owner of Kissner's Restaurant in Defiance, Ohio, for his chicken stock.

Homemade Chicken and Noodles
Karl Kissner

4 pounds chicken thighs
12 chicken bouillon cubes
6 eggs

1 teaspoon salt
4 cups flour

In a pressure cooker, cook the chicken thighs for 30 minutes (or boil in enough water to cover chicken until meat is falling off the bone). Remove the chicken from the broth and set aside to cool. Add bouillon cubes to chicken broth and heat until they dissolve. In a large bowl, whisk eggs and salt together. Add flour until a stiff dough is produced. Place dough on floured table and put more flour on top. Roll out dough with a rolling pin, flipping over as it's rolled out, until it's about an ⅛ inch thick. Cut the dough into rectangular noodles with a pizza cutter. Pick chicken off the bone and shred. Add noodles to broth and bring to a slow boil. Cook until the noodles are tender. Add shredded chicken and cook until chicken is heated through. Serves 8.

───◆◆───

CHICKEN STOCK
Karl Kissner

Whole chicken or 4 leg quarters
1 gallon water
½ tablespoon pepper
1 bay leaf
2 ribs celery with leaves
1 tablespoon salt
1 tablespoon dry parsley
2 carrots
½ teaspoon thyme
1 onion, quartered

Bring all ingredients to a boil in large stockpot and simmer for 2 hours. Strain stock and store in a container in refrigerator or freezer. Makes 1 gallon.

In the absence of chicken, early settlers would also prepare homemade noodles that could be eaten without a sauce or gravy. One of these homemade noodle dishes having cross-cultural appeal to the German Americans, Mennonites and Amish living in the region is spaetzle. A simple recipe typically consisting of few ingredients—primarily eggs, flour and salt—it is an appropriate side dish to meats that have gravy or sauce or a side dish topped with onions and shredded cheese and then baked. Since the German American population of the region also included settlers of Swiss and Austrian descent, the following dish is more similar to the typical Swiss style of preparation, especially if it is topped with onions sautéed in butter and shredded Swiss cheese and then baked in a 375-degree oven for 20 minutes.

SPAETZLE

1 gallon hot water
1 cup all-purpose flour
½ teaspoon salt
1 pinch freshly ground white pepper
½ teaspoon ground nutmeg
2 eggs
¼ cup milk
2 tablespoons butter or margarine
2 tablespoons chopped fresh parsley

Heat water in a large saucepan. Meanwhile, mix together flour, salt, white pepper and nutmeg. Beat eggs well and add alternately with the milk to the dry ingredients. Mix until smooth. Press dough through spaetzle maker or a large-holed sieve or metal grater. Drop a few at a time into simmering liquid. Cook 5 to 8 minutes. Drain well. Sauté cooked spaetzle in butter or margarine. Sprinkle chopped fresh parsley on top and serve.

Snipple beans are made by harvesting green beans when they are a bit more mature than those bought fresh. Beans are put through a snippling machine that cuts them into long, thin strips, similar to French-style sliced green beans. The beans are then placed in a thick layer in a large pan and covered with kosher salt. This continues in alternating layers of beans and salt until all the beans are well coated. Let beans stand for one hour; then drain off the extra salty liquid that has accumulated. At this point, the beans are ready to be placed in a crock and pressed down with a plate weighted with a clean stone or put in glass jars and covered loosely with a lid for storage. Do not cover tightly as gasses will need to be able to escape. Allow the beans to "work" (ferment) for about six weeks. If any scum forms at the top of the beans, scrape it off the top of the liquid that accumulates before using. After six weeks, the snipple beans will smell and taste similar to sauerkraut and are ready to use. In a pinch, already processed French-style beans can be substituted but don't lend the same flavor or crunchy texture to the dish. Cold snipple beans are also a delicious accompaniment to hot German potato pancakes.

Often considered to be part of the Pennsylvania Dutch or Amish culinary traditions, a bowl of rivel soup can be a quick, satisfying winter meal for the German Americans living in what was once the Great Black Swamp. "My mother was not much of a cook," explains Shirley Balbaugh Pickering as she peels russet potatoes for rivel soup. "In fact, I don't remember her making much from scratch at all, except for rivel soup. I also remember my grandmother making rivels." Shirley was raised in the tiny village of Leipsic, in the northeast corner of Putnam County, Ohio, where the majority of residents claim German as their ethnic background. "We were poor," she continues. "I remember my mom opening two cans of Campbell's chicken noodle soup and a can of pork and beans to feed the five of us." Aside from these commercially available foods, rivel soup is one of the few meals Shirley remembers her mother preparing from scratch. She recalls, "My dad had the garden and grew potatoes—rivel soup is basically potato soup with rivels in it to make it heartier."

Rivel soup is prepared by peeling four to five pounds of russet potatoes and dicing them into half-inch cubes and then dicing two onions directly into the pot. "I like mine with lots of onion," says Shirley and immediately adds, "my son-in-law doesn't like onion, but I do—so I'm adding lots of onions." As she finishes dicing the onion, she adds enough chicken stock to cover the potatoes and onions by an inch or two and ignites the flame. Then, Shirley moves across the kitchen from the stove to the opposite counter, where she scoops approximately three cups of all-purpose flour from a ceramic canister into a vintage Pyrex bowl. She continues, "I usually simmer the potatoes and onions for fifteen minutes while I start preparing the dough for the rivels. I usually don't make this big of a pot of rivels, but the whole family will be here tonight."

Once the flour is in the large mixing bowl, she adds a few shakes of salt and black pepper, explaining, "I'm adding the seasonings because the last time I made rivels, they were a bit blah." She cracks an egg into a small bowl and adds it to the dry ingredients and then repeats the process until she has cracked and added a total of four eggs to the flour, salt and pepper mixture. With a dinner fork, she quickly blends the eggs into the dry ingredients just until it forms a ball of dough. She explains, "You don't want to mix the rivels too much, or they will get tough." Shirley likes to use a small dinner spoon dipped in the simmering soup to scoop bite-sized bits of dough from the mixing bowl and place them into the soup. She works back and forth, scooping rivel dough from the mixing bowl and gently dropping it into the soup until all the rivels have been made. Then, cooked, diced chicken is added and the rivel soup is left to simmer for an additional ten minutes before serving.

Rivel soup is a favorite dish for the Pickering family, and the adult children joke with their mom that they would like it better if she'd leave out the potatoes and chicken and just add more rivels. As a child, Shirley remembers her mother preparing rivel soup on a fairly regular basis—once every two weeks or so—and like her mother before her, Shirley prepared rivel soup for her young family on a regular basis. Since all of Larry and Shirley's children have grown and left the house, she has scaled back on the number of times she prepares rivel soup to once a month or so during soup season. As a testament to how common rivel soup is in the predominantly German areas of the Great Black Swamp, variations of this simple yet hearty recipe appear as the soup of the day on menus and special boards at many locally owned independent restaurants.

RIVEL SOUP
Shirley Pickering

4 to 5 pounds russet potatoes, diced
2 onions, diced
2 quarts chicken stock, or enough to cover the potatoes and onions
3 cups all-purpose flour
Salt and black pepper to taste
4 eggs

Place diced potatoes and onions in a pot and cover with chicken stock. Bring to a simmer but do not let boil. Simmer for about 10 minutes while preparing rivels. For the rivels, place flour, salt and pepper in a bowl and add one beaten egg at a time to the dry ingredients. Mix until incorporated. As soup simmers, spoon out rivels into soup. Allow to simmer an additional 10 minutes before serving. Serves 6 to 8.

SNIPPLE BEAN SOUP
Pemberville Historical Society

1 pound fresh pork, fresh pig hock, smoked sausage or ham bone with meat on it
Enough water to cover meat
2 (15-ounce) cans navy beans (great northern beans)
2 cups snipple beans (washed and drained) or substitute French-style green beans
3 cups diced potatoes
Salt and pepper to taste

Cover meat with water and boil until done. Add navy beans, snipple beans, potatoes, salt and pepper and bring back to a boil. Cook until potatoes are done, about 10 minutes. Simmer at least an hour. Serves 4 to 6.

———◆◆◆———

GERMAN POTATO PANCAKES
German American Festival

3 tablespoons flour
¼ teaspoon baking powder
¼ teaspoon grated nutmeg (optional)
1 teaspoon salt
3 cups grated potatoes (about 6 medium potatoes)
2 eggs, well beaten
½ onion, grated (optional)
1 quart canola or peanut oil for frying

Combine first four ingredients and set aside. Put grated potatoes in bowl; add eggs, onion (if using) and flour mixture, beating thoroughly with spoon. Heat oil in heavy skillet. When oil is hot, spoon about two tablespoons of batter for each pancake into oil, leaving about a half inch between pancakes. Cook over medium heat until golden brown and crisp on one side. Turn carefully and brown on other side. Makes 12 pancakes. Serve with sour cream, applesauce or both.

As mentioned previously, many of the early settlers looked forward to relaxing with an alcoholic beverage, and the German community in the Black Swamp was no different. As they planted apple, peach and cherry orchards, settlers would often preserve the fruit they harvested as a libation that could be consumed year-round. One of the most popular alcoholic beverages commonly associated with the German American population is cherry bounce. While the origin of the preparation is obscured, variations of this popular drink were common throughout the colonial era and before. In fact, First Lady Martha Washington documented her own version of cherry bounce on George Washington's stationery.

Cherry bounce is similar to kirsch liquor prepared by German distillers in Germany, but this recipe makes use of simple preparations and local ingredients. The recipe has been around for centuries and was most likely originally prepared using moonshine or other low-quality corn whiskey. In this way, cherry bounce can be seen as an economical way to make low-quality alcoholic beverages more palatable. According to Nick Schroeder, originally from Putnam County, Ohio, cherry bounce can be prepared using tart cherries, rock sugar and vodka, whiskey, scotch or rum. He also makes variations with other fruits. He says, "It's sweet, and you do not drink a lot of it. It is more of a sipping drink" that "compares to schnapps." Schroeder has a large cherry tree in his backyard and considers cherry bounce to have its greatest appeal to older people—"townies"—who give it out for Christmas.

Cherry Bounce
Nick Schroeder

1 quart fresh, unpitted cherries
1 fifth vodka
1 pound rock candy

Put all ingredients in a glass jar and let sit for six months.

Cherry bounce isn't the only alcoholic beverage commonly associated with the German American population in the Black Swamp. Apple wine is common, and some intrepid and engineering folks will distill apple wine into apple liquor.

More commonly, apple pie moonshine is another of these drinks that is intended to make moonshine or other low-quality alcoholic beverages more palatable. Instead of the cherry—which some say has a medicinal taste—this recipe smells and tastes delicious. By taking advantage of the sweet flavors of apple and cinnamon, it can be consumed cold or warm, depending on one's tastes. As far as the alcohol content goes, apple pie moonshine's is relatively low—about equivalent to a strong wine. Traditionally, moonshine was used; however, in the absence of moonshine, one may use a high-proof, commercially available grain alcohol, such as Everclear. One informant said, "The secret of apple pie moonshine is that it's very drinkable, very smooth; it tastes exactly like apple pie. It sneaks up on you because it's so drinkable—you don't realize that you're drinking alcohol."

Apple Pie Moonshine
Kevin Pickering

1 gallon apple juice
1 gallon apple cider
6 cinnamon sticks
1½ cups sugar
1 fifth 200-proof Everclear

Combine first four ingredients in a large pot and heat over medium heat—do not boil. Bring to 180 degrees (use a candy thermometer to maintain consistent heat and not go over) and simmer for 20 minutes. Remove from heat and let temperature drop below 120 degrees. Add Everclear (if using 150 proof, add a fifth and a half) and let cool, covered. When cooled, transfer into glass bottles for storage or gift giving and keep refrigerated. Makes about 2 gallons. Serve well chilled.

Of the Germans who settled in the Black Swamp, there were some who were German Jews seeking opportunity in a new land. The German Jews tended to gravitate toward the larger metropolitan centers, but in the later half of the twentieth century, they started to spread out to the smaller towns and across the more rural areas of the region. With them, they brought their traditions and religious observations, one being Passover.

The Passover Seder is a ritual feast that marks the beginning of the Jewish holiday of Passover. The Seder is a ritual performed by a community or by multiple generations of a family and involves a retelling of the story of the liberation of the Israelites from slavery in ancient Egypt. Seder customs include drinking four cups of wine, eating matzo and partaking in symbolic foods placed on the Passover Seder plate. Matzo is unleavened bread traditionally eaten by Jews during the weeklong Passover holiday, when eating bread and other food made with leavened grain is forbidden according to Jewish religious law.

For the Jaffee family of Toledo and Bowling Green, Passover is an important celebration for which their family and friends gather to celebrate and remember their connection to something much larger than themselves. For this celebration, the matriarch of the family, Edythe Jaffee, developed and prepares the following bagel recipe using matzo meal and eggs instead of flour and yeast to make the bagels light and fluffy.

A tabletop still used for distilling apple wine into apple liquor at the home of an unidentified informant in Paulding County, Ohio. *Image courtesy of author.*

Passover Seder plate of symbolic foods include (clockwise around the plate) matzo ball soup, Passover bagel, dots of red wine, *gefeltafisk*, matzo with *charoset* and a hard-boiled egg at the Leventhal-Jaffee family Passover celebration. *Image courtesy of author.*

Passover Bagels
Edythe Jaffee

1 ⅓ cups water
½ teaspoon salt
1 cup vegetable oil
2 tablespoons sugar
2 cups matzo meal
6 eggs, well beaten

Bring water, salt, oil and sugar to a boil. Add matzo meal while boiling and continue to boil for 30 seconds, mixing thoroughly. Cool a little (very short time) and add beaten eggs a little at a time, mixing well after each addition. With wet hands form 2-inch balls and place on greased cookie sheet (parchment paper can be used instead of grease). Dip fingers in water and then poke a hole in the center of each ball, redipping fingers as needed to keep them wet. Bake at 375 degrees for 50 to 60 minutes (should be brown on bottom). Remove from cookie sheet and place on a rack immediately to cool. Recipe is for 12 bagels per sheet. It is okay to double.

For many of the people living in and around the Black Swamp region, encountering Amish and Mennonite culture is a fairly common occurrence. In addition to the Amish restaurants and stores selling Amish goods, there are numerous retailers offering Amish crafts, furniture and more. While the Black Swamp region of Ohio, Indiana and Michigan is not home to the densest population of Amish in the nation, the region is located between two of the most densely populated Amish areas: central Ohio and north central Indiana.

In the early stages of settlement, the Amish, Mennonite and other German American groups were virtually indistinguishable except for their religious beliefs and practices. In fact, many of the various groups existed side by side, sharing a common language, agricultural practices and culinary traditions.

Today, the frequency with which these populations encounter each other and their shared cultural heritage is more evident in the popularity of Amish baked goods, which are available at more mainstream shopping venues. Like the German Americans in the area, the Amish are well known for their hearty meals and sweet baked goods like pies, cakes, cinnamon rolls and cookies. One of the most popular baked goods is the light, fluffy style of drop sugar cookies made popular in this area by Amish bakers. There are many variations to this popular cookie; I'm only including two to represent the variations.

AMISH SUGAR COOKIES: VERSION ONE

1½ cups vegetable oil
1½ cups white sugar
2 eggs
4 cups all-purpose flour
1 teaspoon baking soda
1 teaspoon baking powder
1 cup buttermilk
¾ teaspoon salt
¾ teaspoon vanilla extract

Mix together vegetable oil, sugar and eggs. Mix in the flour, baking soda, baking powder, buttermilk, salt and vanilla. Do not over mix the dough or you will have tough cookies. Drop teaspoon-sized amounts of batter onto cookie sheets, leaving plenty of room in between. These cookies will puff up and get large. Bake for 8 to 10 minutes at 350 degrees. Makes 2 dozen cookies.

AMISH SUGAR COOKIES: VERSION TWO

1 cup unsalted butter or margarine, softened
1 cup vegetable oil
1 cup granulated sugar
1 cup confectioners' sugar
2 eggs
1 teaspoon vanilla
4½ cups all-purpose flour
1 teaspoon baking soda
1 teaspoon cream of tartar

Combine butter or margarine, oil and sugars in large mixing bowl; mix well. Add eggs and beat for 1 minute until well blended. Add vanilla; beat well. In a separate bowl, combine flour, baking soda and cream of tartar; add to creamed mixture, mixing well. Drop by small teaspoonfuls on ungreased baking sheet. Bake at 375 degrees for 8 to 10 minutes. Makes 2 dozen cookies.

9

Diversifying the Urban Centers

Polish American Food Traditions

B efore the American Civil War, the majority of immigrants arriving in the United States were from Great Britain, Germany and Ireland. This was the same trend in the urban centers growing on the fringes of the Great Black Swamp. However, during the late nineteenth and early twentieth centuries, millions of immigrants migrated to the United States. Many of these immigrants made their homes in the urban centers of Toledo and Fort Wayne. Between 1900 and 1920, there was a boom in Polish immigration to these areas driven by the promise of steady employment in the industrial factories and the opportunity to set up shops where merchants could cater to the needs of the growing Polish community and supply their fellow Poles with traditional Polish products.

Polish national cuisine shares many similarities with other central European cuisines, such as German and Hungarian. It is a meat-centric cuisine using lots of pork, chicken and beef. Polish butcher shops, such as Stanley's Market and Zavotski Custom Meat & Deli in Toledo, are recognized for preparing and offering a variety of cured meats, specialty meats, sausages—such as kielbasa—fresh veal and pork, city chicken and other Polish foods such as pierogi and creamed cucumbers (*mizeria*). A Polish main course usually includes a serving of meat, such as roast or breaded pork or chicken cutlet. Also common are savory stews of cabbage and meat and vegetable salads. Polish cuisine in the Black Swamp is also recognized for its characteristic use of various kinds of noodles, the most common being *kluski*. Popular dishes are *śledzie*, herring prepared

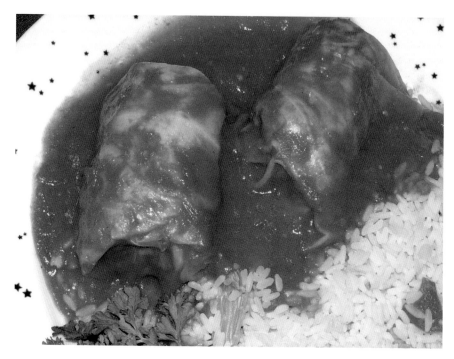

Variations of stuffed cabbage leaves, also known as cabbage rolls or pigs-in-a-blanket, are popular among the Polish and Hungarian communities. *Image courtesy of author.*

in either cream or oil; *kapusta*, pan-fried sauerkraut with fried onions, cooked pork and whole pepper; fried cabbage with bits of kielbasa and noodles; *gołąbki*, stuffed cabbage rolls; roasted chicken with onion; garlic and smoked bacon; potato soup; tomato soup; duck blood soup; and beet borscht. The Poles are also known for their appreciation of beer, sweet wines and potato vodka.

Perhaps the most enduring of Polish culinary traditions is pierogi. Pierogi are dumplings made with a sour cream dough and usually filled with mashed potatoes and cheese, onion and potato, sauerkraut, mushrooms, savory cheese curds or prunes.

Map of the geographic boundaries of the Great Black Swamp. *Courtesy of Kelli Kling, marketing and events coordinator, Wood County Historical Center and Museum.*

Above: Butternuts, also known as white walnuts, are an indigenous nut that has not been domesticated. Like hickory nuts, one must forage these nuts in the wild in order to eat them. *Image courtesy of author*.

Opposite, top: Foraged foods continue to be part of some diets. Here, a wild comb of honey has been built in the window of an abandoned building in Latty, Ohio. *Image courtesy of author*.

Opposite, bottom: Mushrooms are one of the most popular foraged foods in the region. This hen-of-the-woods—*Grifola frondosa*, also known by its Japanese name *maitake*—was foraged from an undisclosed wood lot on a sand ridge in the former Great Black Swamp. *Image courtesy of author*.

Adding sugar to apple butter in a fifty-five-gallon copper kettle at the Grand Rapids, Ohio Applebutter Festival. *Image courtesy of author.*

Master cheese maker Brian Schlatter inspecting a wheel of artisanal cheese in the aging room at Canal Junction Farmstead Cheese in Defiance, Ohio. *Image courtesy of author.*

A Hirzel Farms employee selling fresh cabbage from the back of the vintage Hirzel Canning Co. delivery truck at a fall festival in Pemberville, Ohio. *Image courtesy of author.*

Sauerkraut fermenting in a handmade stoneware crock made by regional artist and Defiance College art professor Steve Smith from Angola, Indiana. *Image courtesy of author.*

Historic general stores such as Beeker's in Pemberville and Olde Gilead in Grand Rapids continue to serve the needs of patrons. This is a detail of the vintage candy counter at Olde Gilead Country Store in Grand Rapids, Ohio. *Image courtesy of author.*

Above: The corn harvest. The Black Swamp region is home to some of the most productive farmland in the nation. Farmers use heavy farm equipment to plant and harvest commercial crops of corn, soy, tomatoes and wheat. *Image courtesy of author.*

Left: Corn remains an important food in the Black Swamp, and many variations exist. This waffle cone of sweet corn ice cream tastes like salted and buttered fresh corn and is from Rita's Dairy Bar in Grand Rapids, Ohio. *Image courtesy of author.*

Fried chicken dinners are a common Sunday meal across the Great Black Swamp.
Image courtesy of author.

Peanut butter pie has a color and flavor combination similar to buckeye candies.
Image courtesy of author.

Szalonna sütés—also known as greasy bread, bacon on a stick and hunky turkey—is a popular Hungarian food presented at the Birmingham Ethnic Festival in Toledo, Ohio. *Image courtesy of author.*

Szalonna sütés prepared at the Tahy family reunion in Wayne, Ohio. The apple wood roasting sticks have been in the family for over fifty years. *Image courtesy of author.*

Above: Pork-A-Lean sandwiches were developed for the Wood County, Ohio Fair but have become popular at seasonal ice cream stands and year-round greasy-spoons, such as the Corner Grill in Bowling Green, Ohio. *Image courtesy of author.*

Opposite, top: Coney dogs are popular across the entire Black Swamp region. While many variations exist, the basic preparation is an all-beef frank, chili meat sauce, chopped white onion, mustard and shredded cheddar cheese. *Image courtesy of author.*

Opposite, bottom: A view through the window separating customers from the kitchen as locally caught yellow perch is hand battered and fried at Jolly Roger Seafood House in Port Clinton, Ohio. *Image courtesy of author.*

Bratwurst sandwiches are popular across the entire region and can be found at most sporting venues, such as Fifth Third Field, home of the Toledo Mud Hens. *Image courtesy of author.*

Mayonnaise-based salads presented alongside pickled beets and pickled beet eggs. *Image courtesy of author.*

Pickle tasting at Sechler's Pickles in Saint Joe, Indiana. *Image courtesy of author.*

Will Oswald proudly displays this tasty cheek meat at a community hog roast. Hog roasts are a popular summer activity centered on food and community. *Image courtesy of author.*

Ben Frobose of Frobose Custom Meats in Pemberville, Ohio, packages venison landjagers for a local hunter. Most local butcher shops offer game processing. *Image courtesy of author.*

Commercially prepared, rolled and dipped buckeye candy from Marsha's Homemade Buckeyes in Perrysburg, Ohio. *Image courtesy of author.*

Locally grown fruit presented at the farmers' market in Toledo, Ohio. *Image courtesy of author.*

Don Schooner pauses for a photo in the community-supported agriculture (CSA) garden at Schooner Farms in Weston, Ohio. *Image courtesy of author.*

Detail of the home wine cellar of Dave Wick, stocked with his homemade fruit, berry and grape wines. Bowling Green, Ohio. *Image courtesy of author.*

Still Life with Eggplant painted by Black Swamp regional artist and Defiance College art professor Douglas Fiely from Styker, Ohio. Fiely paints what he sees: barns, chickens, food and beautiful women. *Image courtesy of author.*

PIEROGI
John and Marge Michalak

2 cups flour, plus extra for kneading and rolling dough
½ teaspoon salt
1 large egg, beaten
½ cup sour cream, plus extra to serve with the pierogi
¼ cup butter, softened and cut into small pieces, plus 2 tablespoons
Filling of your choice
½ onion, chopped
1 cup applesauce (optional)

Dough Directions
To prepare the pierogi dough, mix together the flour and salt and then add the beaten egg. Add the sour cream and the softened butter pieces and work until the dough loses most of its stickiness (about 5 to 7 minutes). A food processor with a dough hook works well for this, but be careful not to overbeat. Wrap the dough in plastic and refrigerate for 20 to 30 minutes or overnight; the dough can be kept in the refrigerator for up to 2 days. Each batch of dough makes about 12 to 15 pierogies, depending on size.

Remove dough from the refrigerator and roll out on a floured board or countertop until it is an ⅛ inch thick. Cut dough into circles (2 inches for small pierogies and 3 to 3½ for large pierogies) with a cookie cutter or drinking glass. Place a small ball of filling (about 1 tablespoon) on each dough round and fold the dough over, forming a semicircle. Press the edges together with the tines of a fork.

Boil the perogies a few at a time in a large pot of water. They are done when they float to the top (about 8 to 10 minutes). Rinse in cool water and let dry. Sauté onion in butter in a large pan until soft. Then, add pierogies and pan fry until lightly crispy. Serve with a side of cold applesauce or sour cream.

The majority of Polish immigrants to the United States brought with them their Roman Catholic faith and many of the traditions common to their homeland. One in particular that stands out as identifying the Polish community is the way Polish Americans prepare for the observation of religious holidays, such as Lent, Easter and Christmas, using food. The Poles living in the Black Swamp region enjoy a variety of sweet pastries prepared at home or in local bakeries. Some of these are nut rolls; poppy seed rolls; Polish coffee cake; *kolachki*, a flaky, folded pastry cookie filled with fruit, cream cheese, poppy seeds or nuts; and *kruschiki*, a light, thin

Pączki are a popular dessert for Fat Tuesday. They are traditionally filled with prune, apricot, black raspberry and apple jellies. More recent variations use Bavarian cream, lemon jelly and red raspberry jelly. *Image courtesy of author.*

dough that is pinched into the shape of a bow tie, or angel wings, fried and then coated in confectioners' sugar.

KRUSCHIKI
John and Marge Michalak

9 egg yolks
3 tablespoons sugar
3 tablespoons sour cream
1 tablespoon rum
1 teaspoon vanilla
3 cups flour, sifted

½ teaspoon baking powder
½ teaspoon salt
1 (32-ounce) bottle canola oil for deep frying
1 cup confectioners' sugar, for dusting

Beat the egg yolks with the sugar until well combined. Add sour cream, rum and vanilla and mix until smooth. Sift together the flour, baking powder and salt and add to egg yolk mixture, a little at a time. On a heavily floured surface, knead the dough vigorously, punching and squeezing as much flour into it as it will take, until the dough is no longer sticky (about 30 minutes). Separate dough into four portions and roll each very thin. Turn the dough and loosen often when rolling. The dough should look like parchment paper that you can see through. Cut dough into strips about 1½ inches wide and 4 inches long. Make a slit closer to one end and bring the longer end through the slit. Heat oil to 375 degrees and fry quickly (only a few seconds) until golden, not brown. Turn only once. Drain on paper towels. Dust with confectioners' sugar.

In the days leading up to Fat Tuesday, the last day before Lent, Polish cooks start cleaning their cupboards of any ingredients that may go to waste or go rancid during the period because they are prohibited from consumption. From these ingredients—such as eggs, butter, oil and flour—the most popular of sweets consumed on Fat Thursday, *pączki*, are prepared. A *pączek* is a deep-fried piece of dough shaped into a flattened sphere and filled with custard or fruit fillings—prune jelly, apricot jelly or other more common flavors, such as red raspberry, black raspberry, cherry and apple. Then, the *pączki* are usually covered with powdered sugar or a sugar-glaze icing.

10

Hungarian American Food Traditions

During the first two decades of the twentieth century, Toledo experienced an influx of another immigrant group, the Hungarians. Fleeing difficult economic situations in their homeland, most of these Hungarians settled near the shipping center of the Port of Toledo, where they found low-paying jobs in factories or as day laborers. In Toledo, the Hungarians tended to settle in their own communities on the East Side of the Maumee River in or near the Birmingham neighborhood. These immigrants preferred to live among people who shared similar cultural backgrounds and beliefs and who spoke the same language as they did.

The majority of these immigrants came to the Black Swamp region with very few possessions but worked hard and saved so that the next generation could live in better conditions than the first-generation immigrants had. Hungarian immigrants who were more successful established businesses that supplied their fellow migrants with traditional Hungarian products. There were an additional two waves of Hungarian immigration into this area. The first occurred after the end of World War II, between 1947 and 1953. Immigrants in this wave settled in with the established immigrants and shared many of the same economic difficulties that earlier immigrants did. Many of these immigrants had few specialized skills and lacked a strong economic status.

The next wave came to America following a failed revolution in 1956. These immigrants also settled among the previous immigrants; however, they tended to be better off economically and were able to establish themselves in businesses and get higher-paying jobs due to their level of specialized skills.

According to Peter Ujvagi—Hungarian-born founding member and executive committee member of the Hungarian American Coalition, active member of the Hungarian Club of Greater Toledo and former state representative of Ohio in the Forty-seventh District representing Toledo and Lucas County—when the old-timers saw this new group getting ahead much more quickly than they and their families had, it bred resentment and the idea that the later groups didn't have to work as hard for what they were getting.

Through the successive waves of Hungarian immigrants, a constant remained their food traditions. Early immigrants and late immigrants alike could socialize and find commonalities over food. One of the most identifying characteristic ingredients in Hungarian cuisine is the common use of both sweet and hot paprika. Some of the more common dishes prepared in the Toledo Hungarian community are *mizeria*, a creamy cucumber salad; *lecsó*, a mixed vegetable stew made of tomato and paprika; *goulash*, stuffed peppers; *toltott kaposzta*, stuffed cabbages; soups; desserts; pastries; stuffed pancakes; stuffed cabbage rolls; meat stews; casseroles; and meats, such as steaks, roasted pork, beef, poultry, lamb and game. The mixing of different varieties of meat is a traditional feature of Hungarian cuisine. Meals are followed with pastries, such as fruit- and nut-filled cookies called *kifli*; strudels filled with nuts, cream or fruit; a layered sponge cake with chocolate buttercream filling and topped with a thin caramel slice called *dobos torte*; a tart with a crisscross design of pastry strips on top known as a *linzer torte*; and many more.

While many of the Hungarian immigrants have achieved economic success and left the old neighborhood for the suburbs and the rural areas of the Black Swamp region, the community continues to support ethnic grocery stores and butcher shops, such as Takacs Grocery & Meats, where multiple generations of the Takacs family have provided the Hungarian community with characteristic specialty meats and sausages, such as *kolbász*, somewhat similar to Polish-style kielbasa; *hurka*, a sausage made of pork liver, meat and rice; and *szalonna*, Hungarian jowl bacon that has more fat than usual breakfast bacon.

Chicken paprikash is a very popular dish and is on the menu at Tony Packo's Restaurant in the Birmingham district of East Toledo and other outlets across the region. Best known for its Hungarian hot dogs—made popular by Corporal Max Klinger, played by Toledo native and Lebanese American Jamie Farr, on the television series *M*A*S*H*—Packo's is often considered to be one of the most "authentic" Hungarian eateries in the region. Chicken paprikash is a thick chicken stew with a sweet paprika cream, or sour cream, sauce typically served with dumplings and a side of creamed cucumbers.

CHICKEN PAPRIKASH
Magdalene Ujvagi

2 to 2½ pounds chicken pieces, preferably thighs and legs
Salt to taste
2 pounds yellow onions (about 2 to 3 large onions)
2 to 3 tablespoons unsalted butter
2 tablespoons sweet paprika, preferably Hungarian
1 teaspoon (or to taste) hot paprika or cayenne
Black pepper to taste
1 cup chicken broth
½ cup sour cream

Salt the chicken pieces well and then let them sit at room temperature while you slice the onions lengthwise (top to root). Heat a large sauté pan over medium-high heat and melt the butter.

When the butter is hot, pat the chicken pieces dry with paper towels and place them skin-side down in the pan. Let the chicken pieces cook 4 to 5 minutes on one side, until well browned, and then turn them over and let them cook 2 to 3 minutes on the other side. (Take care when turning to not tear the skin if any is sticking to the pan.) Remove the chicken from the pan to a bowl and set aside.

Add the sliced onions to the sauté pan and cook them, stirring occasionally to scrape up the browned bits from the chicken, until lightly browned, about 7 minutes. Add the sweet and hot paprikas and some black pepper to the onions and stir to combine. Add the chicken broth, again scraping up the browned bits from the bottom of the pan, and then nestle the chicken pieces into the pan, on top of the onions. Cover and cook on a low simmer for 20 to 25 minutes (depending on the size of your chicken pieces).

When the chicken is cooked through (at least 165 degrees if you use a thermometer, or if the juices run clear, not pink, when the thickest part of the thigh is pierced with a knife), remove the pan from the heat. (If you want, you can also keep cooking the chicken until it begins to fall off the bone, which may take another 30 minutes or so.) When the chicken is done to your taste, remove it from the pan. Allow the pan to cool for a minute and then slowly stir in the sour cream and add salt to taste. If the sour cream cools the sauce too much, turn the heat back on just enough to warm it through. Add the chicken back to the pan and coat with the sauce. Serves 4 to 6.

PAPRIKASH DUMPLINGS
Magdalene Ujvagi

6 eggs
4 cups flour
1 ½ cups water
½ teaspoon salt

Mix all ingredients together in a mixing bowl. It should be a pretty thick, dry mix. If it is too gooey, add small amounts of flour until it is more dry. Pass through a dumpling press over a pot of boiling water. Boil for 5 to 6 minutes. Serves 4 to 6.

CREAMED CUCUMBERS
Peter Ujvagi

4 cucumbers
1 small clove garlic
¼ teaspoon salt
1 teaspoon sugar
¾ cup sour cream
¼ cup apple cider vinegar

Peel cucumbers. Drag fork tines down the length of peeled cucumbers to create long grooves that will look very nice when you slice the cucumbers very, very thin. Put in a mixing bowl. Peel and chop the garlic clove. Add salt, sugar and chopped garlic to the bowl with the cucumber slices. Mix in sour cream. Add vinegar and toss until cucumber slices and sour cream are frothy and foamy. Place in serving dish and sprinkle a little paprika on top for decoration. Serve well chilled. Will keep in the refrigerator for a few days. Serves 4 to 6.

The Birmingham Ethnic Festival wouldn't be the same without the very popular *szalonna sütés*, known locally as greasy bread, bacon on a stick and hunky turkey. The folklore is that Hungarian shepherds would leave town with their flocks and a small slab of fatty yet flavorful jowl bacon. Along the way, they would procure bread, onion, tomato and peppers to be part of their midday meal. Once situated, the shepherd would build a small fire of apple wood and use an apple wood stick to skewer the onion with the jowl bacon above it. As the fire would turn into hot coals, the shepherd would score the bacon in a crisscross pattern and begin roasting it over the hot coals. As the bacon sizzled and fat bubbled up, he would hold the stick at an angle so that the bacon grease would drizzle down onto the outer layers of the onion and then daub the slices of bread onto the bacon grease until the bread was liberally coated. Once there was a desired amount of fire-roasted bacon, the shepherd would remove the stick from the coals and cut off a few bits or a slab of the roasted exterior of the bacon. He would place the bacon on top of the greasy bread and then slip off the outer layers of onion, topping the sandwich with onion, tomato and green peppers. The uncooked bacon and inner layers of onion could then be reserved and prepared for later meals. While the process has been streamlined to make hunky turkey a festival food, at its base, the process remains very similar to the traditional way of preparing this dish.

For the Tahy family of Wayne, Ohio, "bacon on a stick" is a major component of all family gatherings and serves as a way to bring generations together over food. Their family started out in the Birmingham district of Toledo and then moved out into the country, where they started farming. When they gather together to prepare bacon on a stick, there is as much ritual going on as there is cooking. They use the same apple wood sticks that the family has used for over fifty years, and they roast the jowl bacon over a small fire of apple wood. They then prepare the sandwiches using the same process that they have used for decades.

Bacon on a Stick (Szalonna Sütés)
Kathy Tahy

½- to 1-pound slab jowl bacon
1 loaf hard crust Vienna-style bread
1 large green pepper, sliced thin or minced
1 medium onion, sliced thin or minced
1 to 2 tomatoes, diced or sliced very thin

Score the bacon with a knife and put it on an apple wood stick or a long campfire fork. As the bacon cooks and starts dripping fat, have sliced bread on a tray nearby to daub the bacon. Repeat until reaching the desired quantity of grease on the bread. Then gradually add the vegetables to the bread and drip more grease on it. The tomatoes are the last item to add. Be sure to drip more grease over the tomatoes, too. Add a little salt and eat.

11

Lebanese American Food Traditions

Large-scale Lebanese immigration into the Great Black Swamp began in the late nineteenth century and coincided with large-scale immigration into other larger metropolitan areas, such as Brooklyn and Boston. According to Mathew Stiffler of the Arab American National Museum in Dearborn, Michigan, many of the early Lebanese settlers came as laborers in the automotive and support industries developing in Toledo, Detroit and Fort Wayne; however, the majority of the early Lebanese settlers were men who worked as itinerant peddlers until they could make enough money to set up a grocery store, market, butcher shop or tavern and then bring their families over. While they were marked as Islamic Syrians, the vast majority of them were Christians from Mount Lebanon. This wave continued through the 1920s. The second wave of Lebanese immigration began in the late 1940s and continued through the early 1990s, when Lebanese immigrants were fleeing the Lebanese Civil War. More recent immigrants from Lebanon are predominately Muslim.

Vistula was a former village that merged with the nearby village of Port Lawrence in 1837 to form the city of Toledo. This merger explains the irregular street alignment in the oldest area of Toledo, as both villages had platted streets that did not originally meet. When the city was incorporated, these streets were eventually extended to meet at odd angles at Cherry Street. Vistula was one of the more prosperous areas of Toledo, and its many mansions indicate the wealth amassed during the late nineteenth century. However, as the community continued to grow, the wealthy relocated to the Old West End, leaving their ornate homes for more opulent environs.

As the character of the neighborhood changed, Lebanese American merchants and businesspeople moved into Vistula, giving it a new identity as the Little Syria of Toledo. Little Syria encompasses an area roughly bounded by Champlain, Summit, Walnut and Magnolia Streets and became one of America's largest Arab American communities. After World War II, the stream of Arab and Eastern European immigrants trickled off in North Toledo, and the area started its slow, gradual decline.

For decades, Toledo was the home of the densest concentration of Lebanese immigrants in the United States, until an unlikely historical figure caused the population center to shift north to Dearborn, Michigan. Henry Ford was a well-known anti-Semite who didn't want Jewish immigrants working for him in his Rouge Factory in Dearborn, so he actively recruited Lebanese Christians to relocate to Dearborn to work for him. While this caused the population to shift north, there were still many Lebanese communities that remained in the Black Swamp region and continued to contribute to and shape the overall cultural and culinary traditions of the region.

Despite the differences in religion of the various waves of Lebanese immigrants, they share a unified set of culinary traditions characterized by an abundance of starches, whole grains, fruits and vegetables, often eaten raw or pickled as well as cooked. The typical meats prepared in Lebanese cuisine tend to be lamb and chicken. It's also noted for its use of fresh herbs, garlic, olive oil, lemon juice and *za'atar*, a blend of dried thyme, sesame seeds and sumac or oregano, or both.

Lebanese American households and restaurants across the Black Swamp region are distinguished by their characteristic dishes, such as *baba ghanouj*, a chargrilled eggplant, tahini, olive oil, lemon juice and garlic dip; *falafel*, a small, deep-fried patty made of highly spiced ground chickpeas; *shish kebab*, marinated grilled lamb skewers; *shish taouk*, grilled white-meat chicken skewers marinated in olive oil, lemon and parsley; *shawarma*, a sandwich of either marinated chicken or lamb that is skewered on a rotisserie and slowly roasted, similar to gyro meat in the Greek traditional cookery, and then shaved and placed in a pita with pickled turnip, tomatoes and a strong creamy garlic sauce; *tabbouleh*, a diced parsley salad with bulgur wheat, tomato and mint in a spiced dressing; and *baklawa* (similar to Greek baklava), a popular Mediterranean layered filo pastry filled with nuts, covered in a sugar- or honey-based syrup flavored with rose water or orange and then cut in a triangular or diamond shape.

HUMMUS
Beverly Bardwell

1 (16-ounce) can chickpeas or garbanzo beans
¼ cup liquid from chickpeas
3 to 5 tablespoons lemon juice (depending on taste)
1 ½ tablespoons tahini
2 cloves garlic, crushed
½ teaspoon salt
2 tablespoons olive oil
Olive oil, parsley, paprika to garnish

Drain chickpeas and set aside liquid from can. Combine chickpeas and remaining ingredients in a blender or food processor. Add liquid from chickpeas. Blend for 3 to 5 minutes on low until thoroughly mixed and smooth. Place in serving bowl and create a shallow well in the center of the hummus. Add a small amount (1 to 2 tablespoons) of olive oil in the well. Garnish with parsley and paprika (optional). Serve immediately with fresh warm or toasted pita bread or cover and refrigerate. Serves 6 to 8.

TABBOULEH
Chuck Cassis

3 tablespoons fine bulgur
3 medium, firm, ripe tomatoes, diced into small cubes
14 ounces flat-leaf parsley, most of the stalks discarded, leaves washed and dried
2 cups mint leaves, washed and dried
2 spring onions or scallions, trimmed and very thinly sliced
¼ teaspoon ground cinnamon
½ teaspoon ground Lebanese seven-spice mixture
¼ teaspoon finely ground black pepper
Salt to taste
Juice of 1 lemon, or to taste
⅔ cup (150 milliliters) extra virgin olive oil

Rinse the bulgur in several changes of cold water. Drain well and put in a bowl. Stir it with a fork to fluff. Put the diced tomatoes in a bowl and set aside while you prepare the herbs. Using a sharp knife, slice bunches of the parsley and mint into thin strips. Drain the tomatoes of their juice and put in a large bowl. Add the spring onion and herbs. Sprinkle the bulgur all over. Season with the cinnamon, allspice and pepper. Add salt to taste. Add the lemon juice and olive oil and mix well. Serves 6 to 8.

Lamb Shish Kebab
Rhonda Meifert

Marinade
1 teaspoon garlic, finely chopped
2 teaspoons fresh ginger, finely chopped
2 tablespoons lemon juice
¼ cup vegetable oil
1 teaspoon ground turmeric
1 teaspoon ground coriander
1 teaspoon ground cumin
⅛ teaspoon cayenne (or to taste)
2 tablespoons grated onion

Kebabs
2 pounds lean lamb, cut into 2-inch cubes
12 small mushrooms
2 medium onions, cut into large chunks
2 large tomatoes, cut into large chunks

Mix all marinade ingredients in a large bowl. Add lamb cubes and mushrooms and marinate for 1 hour. Preheat broiler or barbecue grill. Divide the meat and vegetables evenly into four parts and skewer the pieces on four metal skewers. Grill over medium, indirect heat, turning to cook evenly for 7 to 10 minutes. Brush skewered meat with extra marinade. Serve with tzatziki sauce (on next page). Serves 4 to 6,.

TZATZIKI SAUCE

1 pint plain yogurt
1 cucumber, seeded, peeled and chopped fine
1 clove garlic, crushed
½ cup olive oil
Juice of ½ lemon
½ teaspoon salt
Parsley to garnish

To the yogurt, add the cucumber, garlic, olive oil, lemon juice and salt. Blend well with fork. Top with parsley. Makes 2 pints.

12

Mexican American Food Traditions

At the turn of the twentieth century, the majority of the Great Black
Swamp had been partitioned, sold off and drained, and the black
loam was producing some of the highest crop yields in the nation. In 1900,
William McKinley, a native son of Ohio, was in the White House, and
the industrialized centers of Toledo and Fort Wayne were teeming with
immigrants from Europe. Yet there were very few residents of the Great
Black Swamp claiming Mexican heritage. The Mexican Revolution of
1910 to 1917 caused many Mexicans to flee Mexico for the United States;
most settled in the American Southwest and found work in factories, on the
railroad or in one of the many industries supporting the railroad. According
to the 1900 U.S. census, there were only 53 people living in the entire state
of Ohio claiming Mexico as their nation of birth. By contrast, there were
206,160 residents claiming Germany as their nation of birth. It would be
decades before the Mexican population in northwest Ohio and northeast
Indiana would grow to significant levels.

By 1920, the rise of industrial agriculture and more efficient food
transportation methods attracted larger numbers of qualified Mexican farm
laborers; however, many of those who came followed the seasonal routes of
the planting, weeding and harvesting cycle. The majority of these workers
were men who would leave their families at home in order to work in the
corn, sugar beet and tomato fields or in one of the many factories turning
out processed foods. Instead of immigrating to one of the urban centers
or the many smaller towns as an entire family, these laborers moved from

place to place across the Midwest with the seasons and would return home to winter in Texas, Arizona, California or Mexico. These workers would not have been counted in the U.S. census.

This pattern started to change in the 1950s, and more families joined husbands and fathers on the road following the agricultural cycle. This allowed entire families to work together in the farms and fields of the Midwest but posed additional complexities to the lives of these migrant workers. While many of the parents who worked the fields had minimal education, they observed the advantages that schooling offered others and wanted the same for their children. Each September, the children of migrant workers would start in school but would not return after the winter break. It was common for the same families to return to the same communities year after year until the father was able to find permanent employment and the family could get out of the migrant lifestyle.

As more and more Mexican men sought full-time, year-round employment in the many factories in Fort Wayne, Defiance, Napoleon, Bowling Green, Pemberville, Toledo and Fremont, they increasingly brought their families and their culture to the Black Swamp region. However, it wasn't until the 1960s that significant numbers of immigrants started to arrive from Mexico and Central and South America. The abundance of rich farmland in northwest Ohio has supported many job opportunities, bringing many migrant workers from Mexico and Texas since the 1940s. For some, jobs are seasonal, but others take root with their families, bringing with them generations of food traditions.

The 2010 census reports roughly 4 percent (30,000 people) in northwest Ohio identify themselves as Hispanic, many of Mexican ancestry. Of this population, over half live in the Old South End of Toledo, where many restaurants, tortilla factories and stores support the vibrant and expanding culture. Of the 288,829 people living in Fort Wayne, Indiana, 3.31 percent (around 10,000 people) are of Mexican heritage or descent. Although small Mexican communities exist in towns like Bowling Green, Defiance, Findlay, Fremont, Oregon, Pemberville and Perrysburg, there is a limit to the variety and authenticity of Mexican ingredients and spices presented at Mexican restaurants in these towns. If one wants a greater sense of the culinary traditions in these smaller towns, it's advisable to take a trip to one of the larger cities on the periphery of the Great Black Swamp region. However, as the Mexican population increases in these smaller towns, the quality of food offerings is increasing.

Mexican cuisine in this region is primarily a fusion of indigenous Mesoamerican cooking and Spanish elements added after the Spanish conquest of the Aztec Empire in the sixteenth century. Before the Spanish conquest, the basic staples were foods such as corn, beans and chili peppers; however, the Europeans introduced a large number of other foods such as domesticated animals for meat (beef, pork, chicken, goats and sheep), dairy products and various herbs and spices. Mexican cuisines vary by regions as does access to ingredients. In the Black Swamp region, the most common regional cuisines presented as Mexican are those of the poorer farming regions of central Mexico (Zacatecas and Guanajuato), western Mexico (Jalisco and Michoacán) and northeast Mexico (Coahuila, Nuevo León and Tamaulipas).

Characteristic dishes are battered and stuffed poblano chilies; enchiladas, a corn tortilla filled with meat, cheese or beans, topped with a chili sauce and served with a side of rice and beans; hearty soups such as menudo, a long-simmered, spicy soup made with tripe and hominy, usually eaten with tortilla or white bread and garnished with oregano, diced onion, salsa, lemon or lime (long considered "the breakfast of champions" in northern Mexico and the American Southwest, menudo is often thought to be a cure for a hangover); and salsa, which refers to an array of sauces typically associated with Mexican and southwestern cuisines. In these traditional cuisines, salsa tends to be of a raw tomato variety with onion, cilantro and jalapeño peppers, commonly called *pico de gallo*, or "cock's beak," and green (tomatillo) salsa. In recent years, new, tropically inspired variations commonly include lime, mango, mint or pineapple. Salsa is often paired with tortilla chips and has captured a significant portion of the American condiment market since the 1980s.

Tamales have been consumed in the Americas for over five thousand years. Traditionally, tamales in Mexico are masa (cornmeal) dough, spread into a prepared corn husk and filled with a spice and chopped meat mixture of pork, beef or chicken. The filled corn husk is then steamed. While most tamales consumed in the Black Swamp region are of the traditional varieties, there are new variations with chilies and cheese fillings that are becoming increasingly common. According to Theresa Rodrigues, a tamale maker in Edgerton, Ohio, "Tamales are a traditional Mexican food. Usually, they were part of a family gathering and holidays, part of the Christmas and Thanksgiving tradition. Usually, [when] the family would gather, the women would get together and have a great time doing all of the work necessary for the tamales—prepping the meat, chopping it. The cousins would play together; it was just a good family time."

Where the pattern of settlement for many of the Germans, Poles, Hungarians and Lebanese was for the man to come to the Black Swamp

Chile poblano, enchiladas and tamales are popular Mexican dishes in Mexican homes and restaurants across the region, as are fried tortilla chips and fresh salsa. *Image courtesy of author.*

first and then bring his family, the pattern for migrant workers of Mexican and southwestern descent was different. Migrant workers tended to move as small groups based on blood relations. And it's not uncommon to see three generations of the same family working the same fields. As migrant workers, women tended to have the greatest level of flexibility when it came to choosing the type of labor to engage in. For example, as many of the families made rounds from farm to farm and region to region, the other workers came to depend on a host of women who prepared food and brought it to workers in the field. For many of these women, selling simple, familiar foods served as an anchor to help the family establish roots in a community so their children could eventually escape the lifestyle of the migrant worker. Many of the Mexican-style restaurants and bakeries across the region had their starts this way.

Salsa
Norma Trejo

4 large tomatoes
1 medium onion
2 cloves garlic, to taste
2 jalapeños, to taste
½ to 1 teaspoon sea salt, to taste
Small to medium bunch of cilantro, to taste
Juice of 1 lime

Bring two quarts of water to a boil and plunge tomatoes into boiling water to loosen skins. When skins split, remove from water and place in a food processor with all the other ingredients. Pulse until reaching desired consistency. Adjust salt to taste. Serves 6 to 8.

Refried Beans
Martina Barrett

2½ cups dry pinto beans
½ cup chopped onion
2 tablespoons (or more to taste) pork lard, bacon fat or olive oil (for vegetarian option)
Salt to taste
Cheddar cheese (optional)

Rinse the beans in water and remove any small stones, pieces of dirt or bad beans. Cook the beans in water.
Traditional method: Put beans into a pot and cover with at least 3 inches of water—about 3 quarts for 2½ cups of dry beans. Bring to a boil and then lower heat to simmer, covered, for about 2½ hours. The beans are done when they are soft and the skin is just beginning to break open.
Pressure cooker method: Put beans into a 4-quart pressure cooker with a 15-pound weight. Fill up the pressure cooker with water, up to the line that indicates the capacity for the pot. Cook for 30 to 35 minutes, until the beans are soft and the skins are barely breaking open. Allow the pressure cooker to cool completely before opening. If there is resistance when attempting to open

the cooker, do not open it; allow it to cool further. Follow the directions for your brand of pressure cooker.

Strain the beans from the cooking water. Add the onions and lard, fat or oil to a wide, sturdy frying pan on medium-high heat. Cook onions until translucent. Add the strained beans and ¼ cup of water to the pan. Using a potato masher, mash the beans in the pan while you are cooking them, until they are a rough purée. Add more water if necessary to keep the fried beans from getting too dried out. Add salt to taste. Add grated cheddar cheese to taste (optional). Beans are ready to serve when heated through. Serves 6 to 8.

FLOUR TORTILLAS
Gloria Pizana

4 cups all-purpose flour
1 teaspoon salt
2 teaspoons baking powder
2 tablespoons cold lard
1 ⅓ cups warm water

Mix all the dry ingredients together in a large mixing bowl. Cut in lard until the flour resembles the texture and consistency of cornmeal. Slowly add water and mix until the dough comes together. Place on a lightly floured surface and knead for a few minutes until smooth and elastic. Divide the dough into 24 equal pieces and roll each piece into a ball. Preheat a large iron skillet over medium-high heat. Using a well-floured rolling pin, roll a dough ball into a thin, round tortilla. Place tortilla onto the hot, dry skillet, and cook until bubbly and golden; flip and continue cooking until golden on the other side. Tortilla can be kept in a tortilla warmer to keep warm and fresh until all tortillas are cooked and ready to eat.

PART III

Contemporary Food Traditions

13

Old and New Traditions

Who Eats This Food?

The foods discussed throughout the previous chapters of this book are often considered to be traditional foods because they tend to be associated with specific groups of immigrants. But what does it mean when "traditional" is used in relation to food and the people who prepare these foods? The word tradition comes from Latin *traditionem*, which means "handing over, passing on," and traditions tend to be built up around sets of beliefs, customs and practices. In a folkloric sense, traditions can be seen as a repeated pattern of behaviors, beliefs or enactments passed down from one generation to the next and a recognized set of present practices with origins in the past or a set of practices created in the past that are purposefully maintained by the group in the present.

Three key aspects to identifying and articulating the conditions through which foods, or sets of dishes within a cuisine, come to be designated as traditional for a specific population are:

(1) Is there a clearly defined notion of who tends to prepare these foods?
(2) Is it widely understood or recognized who commonly eats these foods at home?
(3) Is a specific food or dish used to define the culture based on region, nation of origin, heritage, ethnicity or community associations and linked with the population groups having a history of migration into a region?

Each region of the United States has its characteristic patterns of immigration, and the Great Black Swamp is no different. As the previous chapters show, the richness of diversity in the region has been forged in subsequent waves of immigrants coming to this place and bringing the more portable aspects of their cultures and traditions. These waves of immigration shape and influence our understanding of region and food.

"Tradition is the creation of the future out of the past," writes folklorist Henry Glassie. It is "a continuous process situated in the nothingness of the present, linking the vanished with the unknown." At the core of this notion of tradition is the recognition or sense of continuity between the present and the past. Glassie argues that the character of tradition "is not stasis but continuity; its opposite is not change but oppression, the intrusion of power that thwarts the course of development. Oppressed people are made to do what others will them to do." In this way, Glassie observes that "tradition can be static, and it can be fluid; it can whirl in place, revolving through kaleidoscopic transformations, or it can strike helical, progressive, or retrograde tracks through time." Basically what all this means is that human groups can select specific aspects of their past to pull forward into the present to remind themselves of where they have been, where they are and where they may be going as a people. In sum, tradition serves as a way of organizing the present around the past for the benefit of the future.

Designating foods as "traditional" can be problematic because it calls into question how these foods achieved their status as being traditional and who decided to ascribe "traditional" to these specific foods and not others. Perhaps the most democratic way to go about designating specific foods as "traditional," and therefore carriers of meaning for individuals and groups, is to look at how the food works itself into the local culture and how specific dishes and cultural boundaries expand and change over time. By looking at variations of how the food has changed—how it is personalized, modified and updated for health concerns and socioeconomics—one may better understand the role of this food as a carrier of personal and group meaning. Because if one is willing to update a preparation in order to continue eating a food and preserving a "taste of the past," this food obviously means something. It's also useful to dig into the history associated with a particular food to better understand what this dish originally consisted of and how cooks over the years have updated the preparation for changing skills, access to ingredients and changing tastes.

Many of the foods discussed in previous chapters have specific ethnic and nation-of-origin associations. However, when these foods come to represent and stand in for a region, many of the ethnic associations are deemphasized. For example, to many midwesterners living in the Great Black Swamp region, bratwurst is a midwestern food without specific ethnic or national associations. Since it has always been present during their lifetimes, they might not see the specific style of sausage production as carrying any meaning beyond the everyday. As food increasingly becomes recognized as regional or mainstream, the ethnic associations run the risk of being lost.

What's more, when settlement patterns exist—such as those that shaped the demographic distribution of the Black Swamp region—in which multiple groups of different ethnicities and nations of origin settle in geographic proximity, the likelihood of intercultural sharing of recipes, ingredients, methods of preparation and cooking implements increases. Yvonne Lockwood uses the term "creolization" to describe the varied influences on food production, which brings the discussion up to the question of who prepares this food. Increasing creolization of a food system that takes into account variations that are borrowed from other cuisines muddies the ethnic origin of specific foods and dishes. For example, bratwurst is a traditional German-style sausage, but what happens when one adds ingredients commonly associated with other cuisines into the preparation, such as jalapeño peppers and cheddar cheese? Is it still a German-style bratwurst?

One last question to consider in this section is who eats this food. Eating is one of the most intimate actions a human can engage in because whatever one chooses to consume becomes part of one's body. The forces shaping what people eat are many. Personal tastes are only one aspect determining what one eats; there are also social, cultural, environmental, economic and educational forces at play. For traditional pedestrian foragers, eating their way from place to place, they were less wanderers than they were followers, trailing the seasons in a more-or-less consistent pattern to find various foodstuffs at different times of the year. Contemporary life in the Great Black Swamp is drastically different in that people living here can have the foods of the world delivered to them through the industrialized food system—the average product sitting on supermarket shelves travels two thousand miles to reach the end consumer. But with increasing access to foods across the world, Yvonne Lockwood reminds us, "passing foodways are not regional."

In the contemporary food system, the only barrier between food and eater is access. Access is determined largely by economics. So when one considers who eats this food, it could be anyone who has the economic capital to procure it, the education and interest to prepare it and the desire to eat it. In this era of access to international foods, the distinctions associating a specific food with an ethnic cuisine are reduced in importance. And foods commonly associated with a specific cultural or ethnic group may move from one group to another, or many others. Case in point, sauerkraut is often associated with German Americans, but it is also common in other Eastern and Central European cuisines, such as Polish, Hungarian and Russian cuisines. But who did the Germans learn to prepare sauerkraut from? It is believed to have been introduced to Europe by Genghis Khan, who acquired the knowledge after invading China. What started as a Chinese food moved from being a monoethnic to a multiethnic food in Europe and is now considered to be a regional food associated with the Great Black Swamp.

14

Contemporary Food Production

A Mix of Old and New Methods

At the time of writing this book, Indiana is the sixteenth most populous state in the United States with 6.53 million residents; Michigan is the ninth most populous state with 9.88 million residents; and Ohio is the seventh most populous state in the United States with 11.54 million residents. However, state population only shows a number and not the stories behind those numbers. When one digs into the census data, it reveals that the population of the tri-state region is distributed almost fifty-fifty between urban and rural areas. The largest metropolitan areas are the Toledo Combined Statistical Area with a population of 712,000 and the Fort Wayne, Indiana Metropolitan Statistical Area with a population of 414,315. The biggest area of the Great Black Swamp, northwest Ohio, is home to 1,639,000 residents; yet hard data based on region can be difficult to compile because the Black Swamp is not a clearly defined region of the states of Ohio, Indiana and Michigan. However, the 2010 census suggests that 50 percent of the region's residents live in urban areas while the other 50 percent of the population of the region live in small towns, villages and rural areas.

With all the physical and cultural changes the Black Swamp region has undergone over the decades and centuries, one might think that many of the representational and identifiable foods that have come to symbolize this region would start to be reduced in importance. As more commercially available, prepared foods started to appear on grocery store shelves and as fast-food outlets multiplied in the region and across America, the choice to

The Tomato Gals, contestants for the Bowling Green Tomato Festival Queen, pose with baskets of tomatoes in front of the Heinz Tomato Ketchup Factory in Bowling Green, Ohio, circa 1950. *Image courtesy of the Wood County Historical Society.*

Preparing the tomato harvest to be made into Heinz 57 Tomato Ketchup at the Heinz plant in Bowling Green, Ohio, circa 1920s. This was the world's largest ketchup factory until Heinz consolidated ketchup production at its plant in Fremont (Lower Sandusky), Ohio, in the 1970s. *Image courtesy of the Wood County Historical Society.*

Tomato baskets neatly stacked and awaiting the next harvest on the receiving dock of the Heinz Tomato Ketchup Factory in Bowling Green, Ohio, circa 1920. *Image courtesy of the Wood County Historical Society.*

consume commercialized and industrial food came to stand in as a way of showing unity and contributed to a perception of an overarching national cuisine. The push to establish a national culture during the 1950s by bringing many commercialized foods to rural America had the potential to supplant local and regional foods as the food of choice for many locals. While this may have happened to a degree, many of the foods mentioned in the previous chapters continue to be prepared as a symbolic way of performing group and community associations and identity.

The shift toward industrial food production during the twentieth century in this area was driven because the draining of the Great Black Swamp yielded some of the nation's most productive farmland; yet the economy is split equally between agricultural production and a mix of industry. Fort Wayne is home to dozens of manufacturing companies; notable among these is General Motors' Fort Wayne Assembly Plant. There are also assembly and stamping plants in Defiance, Findlay, Maumee and Toledo, which is the home of Jeep, Champion Spark Plug (Dana), Libby Glass and Owens Corning. Moreover, there are many national-brand food producers across this region, such as Campbell Soup, whose Napoleon plant is the largest producer of canned tomato soup in the nation, and Consolidated Biscuit Company, a contract baker for Nabisco and primary baker of Oreo cookies. Heinz, the Pittsburgh-based ketchup manufacturer, has the world's largest ketchup factory in Fremont, Ohio, and Hickory Farms—producers of specialty sausages, cheeses and snack items—has its world headquarters and production facilities in Maumee, Ohio. Hunts produces its Snack Pack puddings in Perrysburg, Ohio, and La Choy started out in Detroit before moving to Archbold, Ohio, during World War II. La Choy introduced canned Chinese food to many home cooks across the nation. Sechler's is a family-owned producer of fine pickles in Saint Joe, Indiana. The company's private-label pickles are available nationwide, and it produces pickles for other brands, such as Tony Packo's. Spangler produces more than 90 percent of all candy canes consumed in the United States, and it also is the maker of Circus Peanuts and Dum Dum suckers.

To support the commercial food industry, the Black Swamp region has a strong agricultural tradition in which many large-scale farms are dedicated to the cultivation of commercial crops such as corn, soybeans and tomatoes that make their way to these commercial processors. Additionally, there are numerous truck farms where farmers grow crops to sell at roadside markets or markets in the urban centers. Moreover, many rural families tend garden plots to suit their individual tastes and needs.

Since the 1970s, it has become increasingly difficult for local family farmers to make a living off their small farms while engaging in what they frequently refer to as traditional industrialized farming (the regular use of heavy, mechanized equipment, fossil fuels and chemical-intensive farming methods that have become the industry norm since World War II). Many of these small farmers work marginal land that presents a greater level of difficulty to farm in the industrial ways. Additionally, sustainability and land ethics tend to be a common theme in the interviews I have conducted, with many of these farmers engaging in craft or niche farming. In order for farmers tilling smaller tracts, or marginal land, to remain economically viable and support themselves and their farms, many have returned to preindustrial methods, organic farming and niche farming.

Many small farmers across the region offer farm-fresh produce at seasonally operated farm stands. While some of the larger stands may remain open year-round offering a combination of local and nonlocal products, preserves, maple syrup, honey, cheeses and baked goods, there are a large number of small, improvised stands that are stocked daily with fresh-picked produce where customers pay on the honor system. The produce offered at

Candy canes from Spangler in Bryan, Ohio. Spangler is the largest producer of candy canes in the United States. It also makes Dum Dum pops, Saf-T-Pops and Circus Peanuts. *Image courtesy of author.*

farm stands is usually sold at the farm where it was grown. Generally, the market is open daily during the growing season.

Some of the small farms offering fresh produce provide their customers with a lower-cost way of getting the produce they desire: U-pick. This is where the grower allows customers to pick their own produce directly from the field, berry patch or orchard. Since customers are allowed and often encouraged to eat while picking, an entry fee usually covers any produce customers may eat. Despite this, the produce at U-pick farms often costs less since the cost of hiring workers to harvest the produce is eliminated. These markets are typically open every day during the harvest season.

With the increased interest in purchasing farm-fresh fruit and produce, farmers' markets are growing in popularity throughout the Black Swamp region. A farmers' market is a location where several producers cluster together to offer fresh fruits, vegetables, flowers and plants in season. This is a place where farmers have a chance to sell their produce to the public. Offerings at these markets vary based on the venue, number of vendors and the population base of customers supporting the market and reflect their local culture and economy. Their size ranges from a few stalls to several city blocks. In addition to seasonal produce, some markets might offer a wide variety of items such as cheese; meats; eggs; homemade soap; honey; baked goods (cupcakes, breads, pies, cakes, cinnamon rolls, snacks); crafts and cottage goods; jewelry; home wares; locally grown and produced annuals, perennials, shrubs and herbs; garden art; gifts; and local entertainment. These markets are often located in a public parking lot or at a local fairground. Some markets such as Fort Wayne's Farmers' Market and the Toledo Farmers' Market have a dedicated indoor-outdoor venue that hosts a year-round market. During the harvest season, most markets are open once or twice a week. One of the greatest perceived advantages to shopping at a farmers' market is the notion that the customer has a greater chance to get to know their farmers and can cultivate a relationship of trust that translates into added value on the part of the consumer. Additionally, there are other benefits, such as reduced transport, storage and refrigeration and fresher, better-tasting produce.

These shifting attitudes and ethics of land use have driven the growth of small-scale production of food across the Black Swamp region. This shift is probably most evident in the trend toward community-supported agriculture. Community-supported agriculture, or CSA for short, refers to a particular network or association of individuals who have pledged to support one or more local farms, with growers and consumers sharing the risks and benefits of food production. In a CSA, a farmer offers a certain number of "shares" to the public; typically, the share consists of a box, bag or basket of seasonal produce delivered or picked up each week throughout the farming season. Typically, CSA shares consist of whatever vegetables, fruits and other farm products, such as honey, maple syrup, berries, eggs, cheese, meat and fish, are in season and at the peak of their freshness. Some CSAs provide for contributions of labor in lieu of a portion of subscription costs.

Since the turn of the millennium, the Black Swamp region has experienced significant growth of farms offering CSAs to the surrounding areas. One in particular, Schooner Farms of Weston, Ohio, started as a U-pick berry patch that expanded rapidly into a full-scale CSA that continues to draw more subscribers every year. According to Don Schooner, "The idea behind Schooner Farms was to take our little twenty-acre corner of the world and expand our use of it." In addition to fresh fruits and produce, Don and Becky Schooner offer classes on a variety of topics, such as beekeeping, canning, organic gardening, nature crafts, land ethics and more.

Akin to the trend toward niche farming, some farmers working with smaller tracts of land or less desirable, marginal land have experienced difficulty in earning a living off the land. For many of these farmers, they are faced with few options: continue farming as they have been and take jobs off the farm to subsidize the farming operation, rent or sell the land to a farmer running multiple farms or a single large farm or reenvision their relationship to the land and redefine their operation. For farmers like Don and Becky Schooner, this meant going to the community to ask their CSA subscribers to think differently about how they shop for quality produce. For the following farmers, redefining their operations would present a whole new set of challenges and rewards beyond farming.

When the Ralph and Sheila Schlatter family of Canal Junction, Ohio—a tiny village at the intersection of the Miami and Erie and the Wabash and Erie Canals just south of Defiance, Ohio—was faced with replacing costly farming equipment, Ralph decided to convert his dairy over to a grass-fed operation. Schlatter is a fifth-generation Paulding County agriculturalist working the same land his ancestors worked. Instead of borrowing $500,000 to buy new equipment, he decided to cut down significantly on the equipment the operation used. In 1993, he seeded his fields with bluegrass, perennial rye and white clover and turned the cattle in to work the sod.

Presented with the opportunity to make farmstead cheese using raw milk from grass-fed cattle, the Schlatters' youngest son, Brian, a graduate of Northwest State Community College with an associate of science in marketing and retailing management, completed the basic cheese-making course from the Vermont Institute for Artisan Cheese and started using a converted granary to make farmstead cheese. He continued his cheese-making education by working with multiple dairies and creameries in Europe. Today, Canal Junction Farmstead Cheese continues to use the highest-quality milk to turn into handmade, artisan, raw-milk cheese. Brian says his "philosophy is to not only create cheese that is good for you but [that] also taste[s] wonderful. The cheeses take on their own unique taste and attributes that come from the land on which the cheese is produced." His flagship cheese, Charloe, has won awards at the American Cheese Society. In addition to farmstead cheese, the Schlatters sell grass-fed beef, free-range chicken and eggs, bread and other goods from their farm market. They also sell cheese at farmers' markets in Toledo and in other urban markets.

Wine production was introduced to the regions around Lake Erie in the 1820s by early German immigrants who noted the similar microclimate to that of northern Germany and France. The first plantings were Catawba grapes, and by 1860, the Lake Erie area was the nation's leading wine producer. This status continued until Prohibition, when Lake Erie's many vineyards were replanted with jam and jelly grapes. After Prohibition, many vineyards continued with the profitable jam and jelly grapes and were never returned to wine production. By the 1990s, wine production had returned but not on the same level as before. However, regional wines were winning national and international awards, which encouraged additional development of vineyards across the region.

For decades, Mark Schaublin's family has owned the building that he and Lou Schaublin work out of in Gilboa, Ohio. Over the years, it has been a restaurant and a retail store; now, it's a winery, tasting room and retail outlet for their estate-bottled wines. Mark and his friends were interested in making wine for home consumption and decided to enter some into the wine competitions at local fairs. When their product was well received, they started making wine to share and taste among their friend group. As one friend's skill set increased, he decided to plant a larger vineyard and build a winery. Phil and Pam Stotz, owners of Stoney Ridge Winery, near Bryan in Williams County, had offered to buy grapes from Schaublin, until Phil decided that he would prefer the camaraderie of another winemaker in the region and encouraged Schaublin to start producing estate wines under his own label. Stotz's goal was to see six wineries within a short drive of each other so that they could develop a "wine trail," giving visitors a choice of products to sample. In 2010, another winery, Chateau Tebeau, opened near Helena in Sandusky County, Ohio, and there are additional winemakers planning to open additional wineries in Archbold in Fulton County and Grand Rapids in Wood County.

15

Contemporary Foraging

Less About Subsistence and More About Recreation and Sport

For the majority of human existence, we lived as pedestrian foragers traveling from place to place hunting, fishing and gathering for our subsistence. It's only been since the rise of agriculture, horticulture and animal husbandry that human groups have settled down into sedentary communities and started developing the institutions that have come to mark communities such as religion, education, government and economics. What used to be the way of life for all humans has shifted toward more of a hobby for those who enjoy hunting, fishing and gathering for recreation and sport. Since foraging has been relegated to marginal land where agriculture can't take place or where it would be cost prohibitive to work the land, the variety of plant and animal life available to hunt, fish or gather has been reduced. Where the swampy forests and waterways of the Great Black Swamp were once teeming with plant and animal life, the landscape has been altered through deforestation and drainage to better accommodate farming, industry and human communities.

For generations, the fields, farms and woodlots across the Black Swamp have drawn hunters to pursue game for recreation and sport. When the corn harvest is in full swing, they come for white-tailed deer and remain until the harvest is over. At other times of the year, hunters have rabbit, squirrel, wild turkey, pheasant, geese, doves and ducks in their sights. There have even been rare sightings of wild boar, which are most likely attributable to domesticated pigs escaping off the farm. When hunters bag an animal,

Men fishing for walleye on the Maumee River near Perrysburg and Maumee, Ohio. *Image courtesy of author.*

Featured on Friday fish fry menus during Lent, fried yellow perch is popular especially around Lake Erie. It is also popular year-round at restaurants. *Image courtesy of author.*

many local butcher shops offer game processing and will produce a variety of cut meats and sausages out of the wild game.

Anglers travel from surrounding states, or even across the nation, to the Maumee River for one of the country's most sought-after fishing experiences. Walleye are most abundant and easiest to catch when it is warm and the water level is high. Anglers can line up just a few feet from each other on either side of the river and catch the fish with relative ease. Traditionally, the end of March and the first couple weeks of April are peak season, and the run can continue through the early weeks of May. After the walleye season is over, white bass comes into season on the river. White bass season tends to peak around mid-May. During the months of April through June, Lake Erie is a popular destination for white perch fishing, and often, a single fisherman can catch his limit in the morning and have the fish cleaned, battered and fried for lunch. In recent years, fishermen have been able to take white perch from the rivers feeding into the lake. There are many lakeside fish houses offering to clean and fry a freshly caught fish.

There are over 120,000 edible plants worldwide, and around one-thousandth of those end up in markets. Of those, about 30 are the most commonly consumed plant-based foods. With the rise of industrial agriculture, much of the land where previous groups of people gathered their subsistence has been put to the no-till plow, and monocrops have replaced the vast diversity of edible plants. Mostly due to the rise in industrial agriculture, gathering in the Black Swamp is becoming a lost art, so the quickest and safest way to learn foraging is with a local expert. With a little specialized knowledge, a gatherer can learn to spot edible plants where they live, even in a city. There are still many plant-based foods available for gatherers with a keen eye, including mushrooms, asparagus, fiddlehead ferns, milkweed, butternuts, black walnuts, hickory nuts, groundcherries (husk tomatoes), wild onions, wild garlic and various herbs.

16

Eating for Community

For the early settlers to this region, life was a constant struggle against their environment for their subsistence. Life was harsh, isolating and, by many accounts, lonely—especially for women living in the swamp. To ease the isolation and loneliness of frontier life, religious groups, social groups and women's relief and aid groups formed to offer much-needed interaction to their members. Many of the social and cultural activities that contemporary residents of the region enjoy today are very similar to those that were appreciated and enjoyed generations ago. In the Black Swamp region, people gather to celebrate life, death and all the points in between. They gather in community groups based on interests, activities, occupation, neighborhood and beliefs. They also gather to socialize within social groups based on age, interests, accomplishments, skills, heritage, beliefs, neighborhood and so on. At many of these gatherings, food and eating is the primary activity.

Food has long been a device that brings people together, and more often than not, one's attendance at a meeting or event may be determined by the variety, type and quality of food offerings. Think about the stereotype of poor college students responding to the promise of free pizza. Offering food to entice attendance is nothing new; yet the offerings do tend to vary based on the situation, economic ability and the level of skill or interest of the host.

One host who is noted for being above average in all the previous categories was the third president of the United States: Thomas Jefferson. Jefferson brought a new food-production technology back to the United States from an international trip to France. When ice and salt were added to the exterior jacket of a French pot, the contents of cream, sugar and eggs would freeze when churned. Jefferson was the first person in the United States to own a French pot ice cream maker and to write a recipe for ice cream He was also one of the first to host an ice cream social in the United States.

Ice cream socials are used as events to bring groups of people together to not only eat ice cream but also to find a common purpose, whether it be for a school fundraiser, a political gathering or a get-to-know-you event. Ice cream socials are extremely common among church groups, community groups and school groups. While ice cream is the star of the show, there is an added component of non–ice cream desserts such as cookies, cakes, cupcakes and brownies that are brought in by attendees to share with the entire group. In this region, ice cream socials are similar to potlucks, but just desserts.

Potlucks—also known locally as a covered-dish supper—where one is encouraged to bring a hot dish or a covered dish to pass, are social occasions that allow people to come together to share food items, which usually make up a meal. Potlucks have been used over the years as a way to socialize with other friends, family and community without bearing the burden of purchasing, preparing, presenting and cleaning up after the entire meal. Potlucks can revolve around a theme or ethnic food tradition. Potlucks are generally popular among church and community groups. In the Great Black Swamp, potlucks tend to feature shredded chicken sandwiches, cheese- and cream-based hot dips, cheese balls, sauerkraut and bratwurst casseroles, crockpot dishes, beans, hot and cold potato salads, creamy macaroni salads, vegetables, beverages and plenty of commercially prepared and homemade desserts like brownies, cupcakes, cakes, etc. Also popular at these events are pies and pudding-based desserts.

Also common across this region are ox roasts and whole-hog roasts, for which the host prepares and serves a main dish and the attendees bring salads, sides and desserts. Similar to a potluck, some roasts leave the potluck portion open for people to bring whatever dish they would like to share according to their ability; others divide the types of foods into categories such as salads, sides and desserts based on where one's last name falls in the alphabet.

Another popular food-centric event common across the region is tailgating. Tailgating is a pregame ritual people take part in as an act of fandom. Tailgating usually consists of setting up a truck or vehicle in a stadium parking lot prior to a sporting event and cooking food on a grill, consuming—usually alcoholic—beverages and spending time with family and friends. With the number of institutions of higher education across the tri-state region, there are many opportunities for fans to intensify their

Shredded chicken sandwiches are common at festivals, fairs, potlucks, graduation parties and other large gatherings. They are also sold at concession stands and seasonal ice cream stands. *Image courtesy of author.*

team associations through food. Tailgaiting is especially popular at the larger institutions of higher education: Bowling Green State University (BGSU), University of Toledo (UT) and Indiana University–Purdue University Fort Wayne (IPFW). This popular form of pregame socialization has even trickled down to many high school sporting events.

This brings up another eating event that is a common way to celebrate personal achievement: graduation parties. Graduation parties in the Black Swamp region celebrate the accomplishment of graduating from high school. Many families host graduation parties throughout the summer immediately after their student graduates. If the graduating class is fairly sizeable, some families may opt to schedule multiple parties simultaneously to reduce the need for well-wishers to dedicate multiple weekends to traveling from party to party. These collaborative parties often cluster multiple students' parties into a single venue, with a combined menu. Unlike potlucks, the food offerings at these types of backyard events tend to be homemade foods provided by the hosts or catered by an outside source.

Shredded Chicken Sandwich: Basic

1 (20-ounce) can cooked chicken
1 (10¾-ounce) can cream of chicken soup

Pour canned chicken and cream of chicken soup in crockpot on medium heat. Stir occasionally and cook until the chicken has reached your desired temperature. Serve on hamburger buns. May include pickles and mustard. Serves 6 to 8.

———◆◆◆———

Homemade Shredded Chicken Sandwich
Michelle Luthy Crook

2 pounds boneless, skinless chicken breast
1 tablespoon poultry seasoning
¼ teaspoon salt
¼ teaspoon pepper
½ cup water
1 cup chicken-flavored Stove Top stuffing mix, optional

Put first five ingredients in a crockpot on high and let cook for 3 to 4 hours. Reduce heat to warm and shred in crockpot. Add stuffing mix at this time to absorb excess moisture, as needed. Serve on hamburger buns. May include pickles and mustard. Serves 6 to 8.

———◆◆◆———

Corned Beef Cheese Ball

1 (2½-ounce) package chipped corned beef
1 small bunch green onions
2 (8-ounce) packages cream cheese, softened
1 tablespoon Worcestershire sauce
1 teaspoon herb and garlic powder
1 teaspoon seasoned salt
1 teaspoon stone-ground dry mustard seeds

Finely dice corned beef and green onions. Mix cream cheese together with seasonings and then add green onions and corned beef; mix well. Chill overnight. Serve with a variety of crackers.

Dried Beef Cheese Ball

3 (8-ounce) packages cream cheese, softened
3 packages dried beef, chopped
1 bunch green onions, chopped
3 tablespoons Worcestershire sauce
1 tablespoon chives, chopped

Mix cream cheese, chopped beef, chopped onions, Worcestershire sauce and chopped chives. Use hands to shape into a ball. Chill overnight.

Lou Joost's Cheese Ball

2 (8-ounce) packages cream cheese, softened
2 packages chipped beef, shredded
1 tablespoon mayonnaise
1 tablespoon horseradish
2 tablespoons minced onion
½ teaspoon garlic salt
1 teaspoon dried parsley
1 tablespoon Worcestershire sauce

Mix all with hands, shape into ball and chill for a minimum of an hour or overnight. Top with an olive or cherry.

Barbecued Water Chestnuts

1 pound uncooked bacon
2 (16-ounce) cans whole water chestnuts
⅔ cup ketchup
1 cup sugar

Cut bacon slices in half. Drain water chestnuts. Wrap each in a half slice
of bacon and secure with a toothpick. Bake in baking pan for 1 hour in a
325-degree oven. Remove from the baking pan and transfer to a glass baking
dish. Combine ketchup and sugar; blend to dissolve sugar. Pour over chestnuts.
Bake for 45 minutes to 1 hour in a 325-degree oven. If desired, double ketchup
and sugar amounts. Serve warm. Serves 25.

Beer Bread
Sam Jaffee

3 cups self-rising flour
¼ cup sugar
1 stick butter, softened
1 can beer

Mix all ingredients just until they come together. Don't over mix. Pour batter
into a well-greased loaf pan. Bake at 375 degrees for 55 minutes.

Bourbon Balls
Zella Leventhal

2½ cups finely crushed vanilla wafers (about 5 dozen cookies)
2 tablespoons cocoa
1 cup confectioners' sugar, plus ¼ to ½ cup
3 tablespoons corn syrup
¼ cup bourbon, plus a splash or two

Combine wafer crumbs, cocoa and 1 cup of confectioners' sugar. Mix well. Add corn syrup and bourbon and mix well. Form into one-inch balls and then roll in the additional confectioners' sugar. Can be eaten immediately or stored in a covered container for a day or two to age. Can be made as far as a week in advance. Makes 3½ dozen bourbon balls.

Oreo Goodness

1 (8-ounce) package cream cheese, softened
¼ cup butter
1 cup powdered sugar
½ teaspoon vanilla
3 cups milk
2 (3.4-ounce) boxes instant vanilla pudding
12 ounces frozen whipped topping, thawed
1 bag Oreos, crushed

Cream together cream cheese, butter, powdered sugar and vanilla. In separate bowl, mix milk and pudding and chill until set. Fold in whipped topping after pudding has set. Add cream cheese mixture. Top with crushed Oreos. Chill until ready to serve. Serves 8 to 10.

Old-Fashioned Coconut Cream Pie

3 cups half-and-half
2 eggs
¾ cup white sugar
½ cup all-purpose flour
¼ teaspoon salt
1 cup flaked coconut, toasted
1 teaspoon vanilla extract
1 (9-inch) pie shell, baked
1 cup frozen whipped topping, thawed

In a medium saucepan, combine half-and-half, eggs, sugar, flour and salt. Bring to a boil over low heat, stirring constantly. Remove from heat, and stir in ¾ cup of the coconut and the vanilla extract. Pour into pie shell, cover the surface with plastic wrap and let cool for 20 minutes at room temperature. Place in refrigerator to chill for 2 to 4 hours, or until firm. Top with whipped topping and remaining ¼ cup of coconut.

Note: To toast coconut, spread it in an ungreased pan and bake in a 350-degree oven for 5 to 7 minutes, or until golden brown, stirring occasionally. Serves 6 to 8.

Homemade Vanilla Pudding

½ cup white sugar
3 tablespoons cornstarch
¼ teaspoon salt
2 cups cold milk
1 teaspoon vanilla extract
1 tablespoon butter

In medium saucepan, combine the dry ingredients (sugar, cornstarch and salt). Gradually, add the cold milk a little at a time, stirring to dissolve. Then, heat over medium heat, stirring constantly until bubbles form at edges. This prevents lumps. Continue to cook and stir until mixture thickens enough to coat the back of a metal spoon. Do not boil. Remove from heat, stir in vanilla and butter. Pour into serving dishes. Chill before serving. Serves 4 to 6.

17
Celebrating Local Foods

C ounty and community fairs are temporary gatherings where people celebrate local food production, crafts and other goods. Often, they are accompanied by a variety of food vendors featuring an array of fried foods. In terms of foods and competitions, fairs provide an opportunity for the locals to compete for the distinction of having canned the best bottle of peaches, baked and decorated the most aesthetically pleasing cake or crafted the finest bottle of wine. Fairs are about exposing locals to what other locals do in their free time and about celebrating participation and excellence in daily activities. Fairs are also an important entertainment venue for the community and offer musical acts and demolition derbies with cars, trucks, lawn tractors and combines. In the Black Swamp region, tractor pulls are very popular, as evidenced by Bowling Green, Ohio, renaming the town by official mayoral proclamation as "Pulltown, USA" while it hosts the annual National Tractor Pulling Championships.

Foods offered to patrons at fairs tend to be fried, including French fries, funnel cakes, onion rings, deep-fried Snickers bars, deep-fried Oreo cookies and corn dogs. Each fair has its characteristic and representative foods that vary based on the county. For example, at the Wood County Fair, in Bowling Green, Ohio, the 4-H offers handmade milkshakes, the Wood County Beef Producers offer rib-eye steak sandwiches and the Wood County Pork Producers offer the most unique item at the fair, a Pork-A-Lean sandwich: a flame-grilled, whole-hog patty, topped with a choice of shredded horseradish, chopped white onion, mustard or any

Fairgoers waiting in queue for a Pork-A-Lean sandwich at the Wood County Pork Producers stand at the Wood County, Ohio Fair. *Image courtesy of author.*

combination of the three. The producers also offer ketchup for those who want it.

Food festivals are also extremely common, and almost every community across the swamp hosts a festival of some sort. Food festivals can be seen as a longing to make and maintain connections to heritage, place and past. Folklorists Barbara Shortridge and James Shortridge refer to the interest in rediscovering the local that emerged in the late 1990s as neolocalism. They argue that "Americans have paid for their mobile, fast-paced lifestyles with growing feelings of angst and anomie." In short, Americans miss having a sense of community and region to provide an anchor of identity, and small community food festivals are a good way to provide this anchor and sense of place.

Since the largest industry in the region is agriculture, many of the festivals take the shape of place-based food festivals or a celebration of local or regional crops, such as apples, beans, corn, tomatoes, melons, peaches, pumpkins and popcorn. This type of festival emphasizes the role and type

Open-kettle bean soup at the Fayette Fall Festival in Fayette, Ohio. *Image courtesy of author.*

Festivalgoers standing in line at the Northwest Ohio Rib-Off demonstrate how popular eating events are across the Great Black Swamp region. *Image courtesy of author.*

of place-based foods commonly associated with a community. A second type of food festival uses living history to demonstrate a connection of past and present. This type of festival tends to construct and accentuate connections to historically consumed foods, such as locally produced real maple syrup and apple butter as a historical mode of preserving the harvest. In this way, traditional local foods are positioned as part of the heritage of the people who produce, prepare and eat these foods. A third type of food festival common in the region celebrates the ethnic foods found in the area, such as pierogi, bratwurst and apple dumplings. Ethnic food festivals celebrate the community itself by using recognizable foods and dishes to organize notions of ethnicity and identity commonly associated with a specific population. These gatherings also play up the singularity of the local ethnic populations while simultaneously emphasizing their American-ness through sharing food. And finally, the fourth pattern or category of food festival emphasizes the local connection to national foodways through the industrialized, commercial production of foods such as pickles, pork rinds, cookies, wine and beer.

While most food festivals are invented traditions, many find their niche in the cultural landscape by emphasizing foods that are important to the community. Whether the food is grown or produced in the area, the food festival provides a location where food can be celebrated; and eating together in public contributes to a better understanding of how a community envisions itself and communicates the heritage, ethnicity and class of the people who construct the community. In Bucyrus, Ohio, the central food offered at the Bucyrus Bratwurst Festival is locally produced bratwurst sausage. Many vendors offer bratwurst-based foods such as bratwurst sandwiches, bratwurst chili, bratwurst casserole, sauerkraut balls and pita-wurst. In Grand Rapids, Ohio, the Applebutter Festival is celebrated as a way of maintaining established social networks and welcoming visitors while offering a look into the local tradition of cooking apple butter in a copper kettle over an open fire. In Perrysburg, the International Festival celebrates the diversity of the Muslim and Arab American population across the region by offering foods from all the twenty-four to twenty-six nations represented at the Islamic Center of Greater Toledo. In Saint Joe, Indiana, pickles are an important industry that provides jobs and identity to the community. The Saint Joe Pickle Festival offers locals an opportunity to relax and socialize while enjoying deep-fried pickles and a scoop of pickle ice cream.

Men grilling locally made bratwurst to sell at the Bucyrus, Ohio Bratwurst Festival. *Image courtesy of author.*

The Crook family enjoying locally grown steamed corn on the cob at the Corn City Festival in Deshler, Ohio. *Image courtesy of author.*

PITA-WURST
Dixie Striker

1 pound loose bratwurst sausage (may substitute brats in casing)
1 cup chopped onion
1 green pepper, sliced
2 tablespoons margarine
2 cups drained sauerkraut
1 cup sour cream
2 tablespoons mustard
4 pitas

Sauté onion and green pepper in margarine. Remove from skillet. Add bratwurst and brown. Drain if necessary. Add sauerkraut and the sautéed vegetables, and heat thoroughly. Meanwhile, combine sour cream and mustard, mixing until well blended to make pita-wurst sauce. (For best flavor, make two or three days ahead to marinate.)
Cut pitas in half. Open from the cut edge to make pocket and fill with meat, sauerkraut and vegetable mixture. Top with pita-wurst sauce. Serves about 8 using 4 pita rounds cut in half, depending on how full you fill them.

SAUERKRAUT BALLS
Melissa Hill

3 pounds loose bratwurst sausage or hamburger
1 quart sauerkraut, chopped fine
1 cup minced onion
2 cloves garlic, minced
1 or 2 tablespoons butter
½ can beef broth
1 tablespoon minced parsley
5 tablespoons flour, plus ¼ to ½ cup for dredging
32 ounces vegetable oil for frying
3 eggs
½ cup water
¼ to ½ cup bread crumbs

Brown bratwurst, sauerkraut, onion and garlic in butter until meat is gray. Drain well. Add beef broth, parsley and flour. Continue to heat until mixture begins to thicken. Pour on a cookie sheet to cool. May refrigerate to speed up process. Cool until very thick and easy to roll. Roll into golf ball–size balls.
Heat oil to 375 degrees. In a mixing bowl, whisk together eggs and water. In a shallow bowl, pour additional flour, and in a separate shallow bowl, pour bread crumbs. Roll each ball in flour and then dip in egg wash. Roll in bread crumbs to coat. Add to hot oil. Deep fry until brown. Then remove with a slotted spoon and place on paper towels or a drying rack to cool.

The final celebrations of local foods in this book are ones that are not celebrated at a fair or community festival. They are celebrated in homes and offices at specific times of the year: Thanksgiving, Christmas and the annual Ohio State–Michigan football rivalry, known as the Game. Buckeye candy is a peanut butter and chocolate confection produced to resemble the semi-poisonous nut that falls from the official tree of the state of Ohio, *Aesculus glabra* (the common buckeye). Not to be confused with its distant relative, the Reese's Peanut Butter Cup, created in 1928 by Harry Burnett "H.B." Reese, buckeye candy is a bite-sized ball of peanut butter and butter, sweetened with powered sugar and a drop of vanilla and then partially dipped in semisweet chocolate coating. Buckeye candy is both a homemade and a commercial confection. It is as much of a color combination as it is a combination of flavors—brown and tan, peanut butter and chocolate. As long as the color combination and flavor combination remain consistent, a variety of sweets may be produced under the name buckeye, such as buckeye bars, buckeye fudge, buckeye cake, buckeye ice cream, buckeye cupcakes, buckeye cheesecake, buckeye pie and even buckeye popcorn (popcorn covered with peanut butter and chocolate).

Should you choose not to make your own, many local chocolate and candy stores across the Great Black Swamp produce a version of the local treat and even stock commercial alternatives from Harry London, Anthony Thomas and Marsha's Homemade Buckeyes (which is also sold across the nation through Cracker Barrel Stores).

Commercial buckeye candy of the poured variety. Notice the lighter-colored button and poured peanut butter filling. *Image courtesy of author.*

PEANUT BUTTER PIE
Father John Russin

6 tablespoons butter, softened
4 ounces cream cheese, softened
¾ cup peanut butter
½ cup firmly packed brown sugar (preferably dark brown)
1 (8-ounce) container frozen whipped topping, thawed
1 (9-inch) graham cracker crust (below), 1 (9-inch) chocolate-nut crust (below) or 1 (9-inch) prepackaged "Ready Crust"

Beat butter, cream cheese, peanut butter and sugar until well blended and smooth. Gently fold in whipped topping until mixture is smooth and creamy. Turn out into the prepared crust. Refrigerate until firm, about 4 hours. Garnish with cocoa powder or shaved or curled chocolate. Top with peanuts or drizzle melted chocolate over pie, if desired. Serves 6 to 8.

Graham Cracker Crust

1½ cups graham cracker crumbs (about 11 whole graham crackers)
¼ cup sugar
⅓ cup (⅔ stick) butter, melted

Place graham crackers in a resealable plastic bag and crush with a rolling pin. Empty into a medium-sized bowl and add sugar; mix well. Melt butter in a small saucepan or microwave. Add melted butter to graham cracker mixture and blend until the texture resembles coarse meal. Press onto bottom and up the sides of a 9-inch pie pan. Chill the crust for an hour before baking (will help prevent crumbling when serving). For a hard crust, bake for 8 to 10 minutes at 375 for a glass dish, 350 for a silver pan or 300 for a dark pan. Remove from oven and let cool before adding filling.

Chocolate-Nut Crust

6 squares semisweet baking chocolate, such as Baker's Semi-Sweet Chocolate, or 2 (3.5-ounce) Cadbury Dark Chocolate Bars
1 tablespoon butter or margarine
1½ cups finely chopped nuts, toasted

Line 9-inch pie plate with foil; set aside. Microwave chocolate and margarine in large microwavable bowl on high for 2 minutes or until butter is melted. Stir until chocolate is completely melted. Stir in nuts. Press mixture onto bottom and up sides of prepared pie plate. Refrigerate until firm, about 1 hour. Remove crust from pie plate; peel off foil. Return crust to pie plate or place on serving plate. Refrigerate until used.

OHIO BUCKEYE CANDY

1 ½ sticks butter, softened
3 cups creamy peanut butter, preferably Jif
2 pounds confectioners' sugar
16 ounces semisweet chocolate chips or dipping chocolate

Mix together the butter and peanut butter. Gradually add in the confectioners' sugar until completely incorporated. Form the dough into small balls and put on a cookie sheet lined with waxed paper. Refrigerate for 30 minutes to 1 hour. Melt chocolate in a microwave-safe bowl for 1.5 to 2 minutes, stirring every 30 seconds. Stick a toothpick in the center of the peanut butter ball and dip into the chocolate just far enough so that there is still a small circle of peanut butter showing on top. Yields 24 to 48 candies, depending on size. The candy will keep up to 2 weeks in an airtight container in the refrigerator. Enjoy!

OHIO BUCKEYE BARS

1 cup peanut butter
1 cup butter
2 cups graham cracker crumbs
2½ cups confectioners' sugar
10 ounces milk chocolate chips
6 tablespoons cooking oil

Add peanut butter and butter to a microwave-safe bowl and soften in the microwave for 30 or so seconds. Mix together. Stir in the graham cracker crumbs and confectioners' sugar. Mix well. Pat mixture into bottom of a 9- by 13-inch pan. On low heat, melt the chocolate chips in a microwave. Stir in the cooking oil. Pour over crust and refrigerate for several hours. Cut into bars and enjoy! Makes around 24 bars.

Bibliography

Anderson, Benedict. *Imagined Communities: Reflections on the Origin and Spread of Nationalism*. London: Verso, 1983, 1991.

Barth, Fredrik. "Ethnic Group and Boundaries." *Theories of Ethnicity: A Classical Reader*. Edited by Werner Sollors. Washington Square: New York University Press, 1996.

Bell, David, and Gill Valentine. *Consuming Geographies: We Are Where We Eat*. London: Routledge, 1997.

Ben-Amos, Dan. "The Seven Strands of Tradition: Varieties in Its Meaning in American Folklore Studies." *Journal of Folklore Research* 21, no. 2–3 (1984): 97–131.

Brown, Linda Keller, and Kay Mussell, eds. *Ethnic and Regional Foodways in the United States: The Performance of Group Identity*. Knoxville: University of Tennessee Press, 1984.

Buchman, Randall. "The Seneca-Cayuga." The Conference on Indian Removal from Ohio: As a Result of the Impact of the War of 1812. May 10–12, 2012.

Camp, Charles. *American Foodways: What, When, Why, and How We Eat in America*. Little Rock, AR: August House, 1989.

Crook, Nathan. "Foods That Matter: Constructing Place and Community at Food Festivals in Northwest Ohio." Electronic thesis or dissertation, Bowling Green State University, 2009. OhioLINK Electronic Theses and Dissertations Center. September 11, 2013.

De Wit, Cary W. "Food-Place Associations on American Product Labels." Chap. 8 in *The Taste of American Place: A Reader on Regional and Ethnic Foods.* Edited by Barbara G. Shortridge and James R. Shortridge. Lanham, MD: Rowman & Littlefield, 1998.

Dreimanis, Aleksis. "Late Wisconsin Glacial Retreat in the Great Lakes Region, North America." *Annals of the New York Academy of Sciences* 288 (n.d.): 70–89.

Fletcher, Lyle R. "A Brief History of Wood County, Ohio." In *Bowling Green, Ohio: A Sequicentennial History, 1833–1983.* Bowling Green, OH: Bowling Green Sequicentennial Commission, 1995, 236–38.

Gabaccia, Donna. *We Are What We Eat: Ethnic Food and the Making of Americans.* Cambridge, MA: Harvard University Press, 1998.

Glassie, Henry. "The Spirit of Swedish Folk Art." Epilogue in *Swedish Folk Art: All Tradition Is Change.* Edited by Barbro Klein and Mats Widbom. New York: Abrams and Kulturhuset, 1994.

———. "Tradition." Chap. 7 in *Eight Words for the Study of Expressive Culture.* Edited by Burt Feintuch. Urbana: University of Illinois Press, 2003.

Goody, Jack. "Industrial Food: Towards the Development of a World Cuisine." Chap. 5 in *Cooking, Cuisine and Class.* Cambridge, UK: Cambridge University Press, 1982.

Green, W.J., Paul Thayer and J.B. Keil. "Varieties of Apples in Ohio." Bulletin of the Ohio Agricultural Experiment Station. Wooster: Ohio State University, 1915.

Havighurst, Walter. *Ohio: A History.* Urbana: University of Illinois Press, 2001.

Heldke, Lisa. *Exotic Appetites: Ruminations of a Food Adventurer.* New York: Routledge, 2003.

Howe, Henry. *Historical Collections of Ohio.* Cincinnati, OH: H. Howe at E. Morgan & Co.'s, 1851.

Jones, Michael Owen. "Food Choice, Symbolism, and Identity: Bread-and-Butter Issues for Folkloristics and Nutrition Studies (American Folklore Society Presidential Address, October 2005)." *Journal of American Folklore* 120, no. 476 (Spring 2007): 129–77.

Kaatz, M.R. "The Black Swamp: A Study in Historical Geography." *Annals of the Association of American Geographers* 45, no. 1 (1955): 1–35.

Kamphoefner, Walter. Interview by Jennifer Ludden. National Public Radio. April 1, 2009. Accessed September 11, 2013.

Keller, Robert H. "America's Native Sweet: Chippewa Treaties and the Right to Harvest Maple Sugar." *American Indian Quarterly* 13, no. 2 (Spring 1998): 117–35.

Knepper, George W. *The Official Ohio Lands Book*. Columbus: State Auditor of Ohio, 2002.

————. *Ohio and Its People: Bicentennial Edition*. Kent, OH: Kent State University Press, 2003.

Lang, William. *History of Hancock County, Ohio*. Chicago: Warner, Beers and Co., 1886.

————. *History of Seneca County, Ohio*. Chicago: Warner, Beers and Co., 1886.

Lockwood, Yvonne R., and William G. Lockwood. "Pasties in Michigan's Upper Peninsula: Foodways, Interethnic Relations, and Regionalism." Chap. 1 in *The Taste of American Place: A Reader on Regional and Ethnic Foods*. Edited by Barbara G. Shortridge and James R. Shortridge. Lanham, MD: Rowman & Littlefield, 1998.

Long, Lucy M. *Culinary Tourism*. Lexington: University of Kentucky Press, 2004.

————. "Green Bean Casserole and Midwestern Identity: A Regional Foodways Aesthetic and Ethos." *Midwestern Folklore* 33, no. 1 (2007): 32, 39–40.

————. "Myths and Folklore." *Oxford Companion to American Food and Drink*. Edited by Andrew F. Smith. New York: Oxford University Press, 2007.

————. *Regional American Food Cultures*. Santa Barbara, CA: Greenwood Press, 2009.

————. *Stirring Up the Past: The Grand Rapids Applebutter Fest*. Bowling Green, OH: WBGU, 2006.

Lossing, Benson J. *Pictorial Field Book of the War of 1812*. New York: Harper and Brothers Publishers, 1868.

Nearing, Helen, and Scott Nearing. *The Maple Sugar Book*. New York: John Day, 1950.

Ohio Proud: Made in Ohio Grown in Ohio. http://www.ohioproud.org.

Parish, John C., ed. "The Robert Lucas Journal of the War of 1812 During the Campaign Under General William Hull." Iowa City: State Historical Society of Iowa, 1906.

Pollan, Michael. Interview by Gwen Ifill. PBS NewsHour. June 29, 2001. http://www.pbs.org/newshour/bb/entertainment/jan-june01/botany_06-29.html.

Preston, H.L. *Dirt Roads to Dixie: Accessibility and Modernization in the South, 1885–1935*. Knoxville: University of Tennessee Press, 1991.

Shortridge, Barbara G., and James R. Shortridge. "Food and American Culture." Introduction in *The Taste of American Place: A Reader on Regional and Ethnic Foods*. Edited by Barbara G. Shortridge and James R. Shortridge. Lanham, MD: Rowman & Littlefield, 1998.

Slocum, Charles E. "History of the Maumee River Basin from the Earliest Account to Its Organization into Counties." *Journal of the Maumee Valley Pioneer Association*. Toledo, OH: Bowen and Slocum, 1901.

"Treaty of the Maumee Rapids (1817) (Transcript)." Ohio History Central. July 1, 2005. http://www.ohiohistorycentral.org/entry.php?rec=440.

Trubek, Amy. *The Taste of Place: A Cultural Journey into Terroir*. Berkeley: University of California Press, 2008.

White, Jonathan W., and J. Clyde Underwood. "Maple Syrup and Honey." *Symposium of the American Chemical Society: Sweeteners*. Edited by G.E. Inglett et al. Westport, CT: AVI Publishing Co., 1974.

Winter, Nevin O. *A History of Northwest Ohio: A Narrative Account of Its Historical Progress and Development from the First European Exploration of the Maumee and Sandusky Valleys and the Adjacent Shores of Lake Erie, Down to the Present Time*. Chicago: Lewis Publishing Company, 1917.

Index

About the Author

Nathan C. Crook is a cultural anthropologist and assistant professor of English and agricultural communication at The Ohio State University's agricultural campus located in Wooster on the northern end of Ohio's Amish Country. He holds a PhD in American cultural studies from Bowling Green State University in Bowling Green, Ohio. Crook researches and writes about the myriad uses of food as a community identifier and a mode of communication. While Crook's research is interdisciplinary, his primary area of focus is on the use of the ephemeral as a communicative device in daily life. His doctoral dissertation examines the historical, social and cultural role of foods presented at food festivals in northwest Ohio. In addition to his research and writing about midwestern culinary history and food traditions, he has conducted original fieldwork internationally and domestically, focusing on southern Italian and Sicilian regional cultures and cuisines and those of the Intermountain West and the Pacific Northwest. In addition to this book on the culinary history of the Black Swamp region, Dr. Crook has published numerous articles on local and regional foods, food traditions, practices and patterns of behavior with the Culinary Historians of Ann Arbor, the Ohio Humanities Council and the Oxford University Press.

Photo courtesy Michelle L. Crook.